HEARST MARINE BOOKS
GUIDE TO SALTWATER FISHING BOATS

HEARST MARINE BOOKS
GUIDE TO SALTWATER FISHING BOATS

Joe Skorupa

Illustrations by Ron Carboni
Photographs by Joe Skorupa

HEARST MARINE BOOKS
New York

Library of Congress Cataloging-in-Publication Data

Skorupa, Joe.
    Hearst Marine Books guide to saltwater fishing boats / by Joe Skorupa.
        .p.   cm.
    Includes index.
    ISBN 0-688-13414-9
    1. Fishing boats—Design and construction.   2. Fishing boats—Equipment and supplies.   3. Saltwater fishing—Equipment and supplies.   I. Title.   II. Title: Guide to saltwater fishing boats.
VM431.S58   1994
799.1'6—dc20   94-18809
                                                                                          CIP

Printed in the United States of America

First Edition

1 2 3 4 5 6 7 8 9 10

ACKNOWLEDGMENTS

A couple of years ago, Michael Mouland, the editor at William Morrow and Co. who handles Hearst Marine Books, convinced me that a new book was needed on the subject of trailer boating, and that I was the right person to write it. Frankly, it didn't take much convincing. I was anxious to write a book at the time. After finishing the book, however, I needed considerably more convincing to write a second one. The task turned out to be far more arduous (and rewarding) than anticipated. Somehow, Michael indeed convinced me to take on a second project, and this is the result. Again, it was more difficult than expected, and in the end, more rewarding. Thanks for the opportunity, Michael.

I would also like to thank a close friend and colleague, Dean Travis Clarke, who somehow found the time to proofread my manuscript. As executive editor of *Sportfishing* magazine, Dean has been there and done that as much as anyone in saltwater angling, and his help was invaluable.

Three others provided support that also contributed to this book. The first is renowned fisherman and writer Al Ristori, a fellow New Jerseyan. I've spent several weeks fishing with Al over the years, and have come to regard his knowledge of saltwater gamefish as encyclopedic. His two books, *North American Saltwater Fishing* and *Gamefish of North America,* are wonderful resources and provided me with useful insights, especially for background research for Chapter 8. A second supporter of this project was Joe Oldham, the editor-in-chief at *Popular Mechanics* (my day job). I am indebted to Joe not only for providing me with the kind of environment that allows me to pursue projects like this, but for inspiring me to aim for the highest of standards in writing, artwork, and photography. A more direct contributor to this book is artist Ron Carboni. I've worked with Ron many times over the years, and his illustrations become better with each project. For proof, check out Ron's work in Chapter 8.

Finally, I would like to express gratitude to my wife, Robin, who was more supportive of a late-night and weekend writing schedule than I ever could have expected. I couldn't have completed this book, or the first one for that matter, without Robin's guidance, patience, confidence, and overall support. I am truly in her debt, and it is my greatest pleasure to make every effort to repay it.

CONTENTS

ACKNOWLEDGMENTS

v

INTRODUCTION

ix

CHAPTER 1

THE ART OF THE
SALTWATER FISHING BOAT

1

CHAPTER 2

VERSATILE CENTER CONSOLES

15

CHAPTER 3

MIDSIZE WALKAROUNDS
AND CUDDY CABINS

29

CHAPTER 4

BATTLE WAGONS:
CONVERTIBLE SPORTFISHERMEN

41

CHAPTER 5

FLATS BOATS, EXPRESS BOATS, AND
OTHER HYBRIDS

55

CONTENTS

CHAPTER 6
OUTFITTING: ELECTRONICS, EQUIPMENT, ACCESSORIES
69

CHAPTER 7
BOAT HANDLING AND MAINTENANCE
81

CHAPTER 8
SALTWATER GAMEFISH IDENTIFIER
93

GLOSSARY
111

INDEX
121

INTRODUCTION

The excitement of offshore fishing starts before dawn in the cool, briny air as you load the boat with food, bait, and gear. It continues to build as you watch the sun rise through the mangroves on the way to open water. Navigating through the channel, you see the waves stacking up in the distance, the first sign of the approaching Gulf Stream. When you finally lose sight of land, you take a deep breath. You're in one of the best sportfishing grounds in the world and conditions couldn't be better.

With nothing but blue-green horizon in all directions, you rig lines, bait hooks, and set rods in place. All eyes scan the water for signs of fish. Then, a line dances and a reel begins to sing. An underwater battler makes a furious run, and your mind races along with it: Will the fish jump or sound? Will it throw the hook? Snap the line? Spool the reel? Will it be a keeper or a releaser? More thoughts follow in a flash and continue as you begin to muscle in line. The clash can last anywhere from minutes to hours,

but one thing is certain. Every second will be an unforgettable, pulse-pounding thrill.

My first offshore fishing adventure was modest in all aspects. It was fifteen years ago. Out of Key West, Florida. We were in a small, trailerable walkaround cabin boat and caught little more than cero mackerel and tripletail. Oh, I hooked up with a sailfish, but it threw the hook on the third jump. I brought a dolphin to boat, but it snapped the line before being hoisted aboard. Some might say this was a trip of lost opportunities, but I wouldn't. A hook was set that day, and the invisible line has pulled me back ever since.

Following that memorable Key West adventure, I've spent hundreds of days on saltwater fishing boats, both in the shallows and offshore. I've been out on walkaround cabins, center consoles, cuddy cabins, convertibles, flats boats, bay boats, expresses, dual consoles, and what I call hybrids—rigs that combine features from several different designs. And while these boats are all very different from one another, they have one thing in common—they're purebred saltwater fishing machines in both design and intent.

Without question, there's a lot to appreciate about a well-built saltwater fishing rig. First, there's ruggedness. The pounding, corrosive saltwater environment doesn't take kindly to poorly made boats. Second, modern saltwater fishing rigs are masterworks of what I call sport-specific design. Although offshore center-console boats may appear to be similar to flats boats, they're actually very different animals. The same is true of flybridge boats and convertibles (which can appear similar except for size), and for open expresses and cuddy cabin boats.

These boats are different from one another in fundamental ways, such as hull shape, profile, and layout, and in important features, such as bait stations, dual helm controls, bait wells, casting platforms, outriggers, cockpit layout, aluminum towers, and many others. *Hearst Marine Books Guide to Saltwater Fishing Boats* not only identifies these differences, but tells you what functions they serve from both a designer's and a fisherman's point of view. The book tells you why an element or feature is designed the way it is, and how it's intended to be used. It also covers the basics of outfitting an offshore fishing rig with cutting-edge accessories, equipment, and electronics. And, in two important sections, it provides a look into the fundamentals of state-of-the-art boat building and construction, and offers helpful tips for crucial money-saving saltwater maintenance.

Not long ago, a book like this one would have been a slim volume. Fishing boats through the 1970s, with several exceptions, were bare-bones, all-purpose rigs. Fishermen generally bought a V-bottom platform and added everything else later. But like the automotive industry, the boating industry has become increasingly sophisticated in recent years. It has moved away from one-design-fits-all to rigs that fulfill highly specific requirements. Today's boats are not only designed specifically for fishing on the flats, the inshore bays, or the open ocean, but also for a particular species of fish. I call this approach sport-specific design, and it's clearly the most important trend to occur in boat building in the past decade.

The *Guide to Saltwater Fishing Boats* presents everything you need to know about this trend in a well-illustrated, easy-to-read manner that's spiced with tidbits of historical perspective on one of the world's most colorful sports. The book is an essential resource for novices buying their first boats, veteran fishermen trading in older rigs for newer ones, and anyone interested in outfitting a saltwater fishing boat with the latest custom or aftermarket gear. It bristles with tips that help offshore fishermen maximize their boating time, fishing efficiency, and monetary investment. A glossary in the back of the book highlights important terms for easy reference, and in one of the most useful chapters, a fish identifier provides information on the ranges and seasons for catching fish in the Gulf of Mexico, and the Atlantic and Pacific oceans (both inshore and offshore).

Fifteen years after my trip to Key West, I've come to realize that a well-built saltwater fishing boat isn't just a platform from which to catch fish, but a ticket to the most exciting sport in the world.

HEARST MARINE BOOKS
GUIDE TO SALTWATER FISHING BOATS

CHAPTER 1

THE ART OF THE SALTWATER FISHING BOAT

Presented with an offer few of us could refuse, Ernest Hemingway, of course, did just that. It was the late 1950s and some Cuban friends noticed that Hemingway's fishing boat, *Pilar,* was well past her prime. They talked it over among themselves and decided it was time the celebrated sportfisherman moved beyond his modified twenty-five-year-old trunk-cabin commuter to a state-of-the-art battle wagon. At a party in Havana, the friends presented Hemingway with a gift. It was a slip of paper authorizing him to pick out any boat he wanted, free of charge.

As noted, the Nobel Prize–winning author politely refused the generous offer. He pointed out that *Pilar* had been good to him in the past, and it would be good to him in the future. In fact, if he couldn't fish on *Pilar,* he said, he wouldn't fish at all. And so it was. Hemingway took his life a few years later, and true to his word, *Pilar* was the only boat he owned.

Some say that Hemingway's deep loyalty to the thirty-eight-foot, black-hulled boat, which was built in 1934 by Wheeler Brothers, of the Bronx, New York, was partly due to his calling it *Pilar.* This was reportedly the name he had chosen for the daughter he never had. Another reason for loyalty was that *Pilar* had been very good to her owner. On Hemingway's first day out on her, he caught eighteen dolphin, an enviable feat both then and now. And for three decades, she regularly fished the waters between the Florida Keys, Cuba, and the Bahamas, enabling Hemingway to set several world records, including catching seven marlin in one day.

Perhaps the final reason Hemingway remained true to *Pilar* was that the wooden-hulled, twin-engine rig (fitted with a 75-horse Chrysler main and a 40-horse Lycoming troller) was custom-built to his specifications and modified over the years according to his design. She was literally everything he wanted, and, make no mistake about it: *Pilar* was

1

Ernest Hemingway and his celebrated fishing boat, Pilar, which pioneered many of the techniques and components used on modern fishing rigs.

the leading midsize fishing boat in her day.

But great strides had been made in boat design and construction since 1934, and they accelerated during the years following World War II. No doubt, if most of us had been offered Hemingway's deal—trading in an old vintage warhorse for a new, cutting-edge fishing machine—we'd have accepted it in a flash.

This is especially true when you place the offer in context. Keep in mind that when Hemingway purchased *Pilar,* the only features and equipment on the boat were twin engines, a fish box in the stern, a live-bait well, several stowage compartments, an open aft cockpit, and a cabin with six berths, an alcohol stove, two heads, and a dinette. Hemingway immediately added a compass and a good timepiece for navigation, and a chair for fighting fish. (Not a dedicated fighting chair, mind you, but simply a chair placed in the boat.) So much for accessories.

Before World War II, as new developments arrived on the fishing scene, Hemingway added gaffs, outriggers (which he pioneered), rod holders, and rollers to aid in sliding big fish over the side. After the war, he added a true fighting chair and a small aluminum tower. Both of these were installed at Rybovitch Boats, in Palm Beach, Florida, soon to become the leading boatyard of the second half of this century for custom saltwater fishing rigs.

By the time Hemingway abandoned Cuba in 1960, advancements in fishing boats had left *Pilar*'s technology far behind. These developments included fiberglass construction, deep-V and planing hulls, multistory tuna towers, VHF radios, and sonar units that could read bottom contours and locate fish. Soon to come were other important advancements, including Sat/Com radios, loran navigators, radar for small boats, electronic plotters, counter-rotating props for dual-engine installations, and such now-familiar boat designs as center consoles, walkaround cabins, and flats boats.

The pace of advancement, if anything, has only increased in recent years, and today's fishermen can take advantage of numerous new developments that make the modern fishing boat more durable, reliable, and efficient, plus safer and easier to maintain.

HULL CONSTRUCTION

As mentioned, Hemingway's boat was made of wood (steam-bent white oak). Its hull was painted black and its deck was varnished. For boats like this, maintenance was never-ending. By the late 1940s, a dramatic innovation in boat building and hull construction changed all that. It was called **fiberglass,*** and soon after it arrived on the scene, it revolutionized boat building. Today, few fishing boats are made of wood.

Some of the early proponents of fiberglass were angry at its name. They were angry because the new material was nothing like glass. They said, "*fiberiron* or *fibersteel* would be a more descriptive name," and they were right. Fiberglass is virtually indestructible in normal use, a fact that's now become a sore point to builders. Today, instead of extolling the virtues of fiberglass, you're more likely to hear them say: "The damn stuff won't wear out."

So what is this miracle substance? Fiberglass is a composite plastic made from resins and polyester or glass fibers. Technically, it's known as fiberglass reinforced plastic. Unlike wood, aluminum, or steel, fiberglass isn't a homogeneous material. It's a multilayered and bonded material that's similar in construction to a sheet of plywood. Each fiberglass-boat builder has its own ideas about the best materials to use and how best to use them, but once bonded together into a finished material called a **laminate,** fiberglass has amazing strength.

Laminates are added to the hull mold layer by layer, starting with the exterior gel coat first. The final touches to the hull mold are the stringer system, which gives the finished boat strength and integrity.

Fiberglass boat building begins with an empty **mold,** which is a carefully constructed hollow cavity. A boat mold is actually a mirror image of the boat's final shape. It's based on a wooden or clay model that's typically designed by a naval architect. Original models are built to exacting specifications and polished to flawless perfection. When the model is finished, a mold is cast. In this way, the model's exact shape and smooth surface are transferred to the mold, which then transfers them to the finished component. Components typically made from molds are hulls, topside superstructures, helm areas, decks, below-decks cabins, and **inner liners**, those intermediate pieces between the belowdecks cabin and the hull. Molds for each of these components are highly individual and proprietary to each builder. Essentially, they are the heart of a builder's business.

The first thing a boat builder does to a mold is to wax the interior surface. The wax ensures that the finished hull will pop out without damaging the

newly created piece or the mold itself—an equally important factor. Then, the builder begins adding each layer of laminate material, either by sprayup using a so-called chopper gun, or layup by hand. This is done in reverse order, from the outside in. Remember, the inner wall of the mold is the shape of the outer surface of the finished piece.

Liquid substances that bind the laminate materials together into a solid are called **resins.** In boat building, resins typically used are of the polyester type, which means they harden or **cure** through a chemical reaction caused by a catalyst. This chemical reaction releases heat, thus giving these resins the family name **thermosetting.** Those of us not familiar with fiberglass may know something about another family of resins called epoxy resins. These are rarely used in boat building because of their two-part nature (one part resin, one part hardener), which makes them difficult to work with in large-scale construction.

The first layer of laminate material applied to the mold is called **gel coat,** which is a combination of resin and pigment. Gel coat is applied by spray gun to the mold. If colors or stripes appear on the outer surface, these are the first elements put in place. Once the gel coat cures to a sufficient hardness (but not complete solidity), each consecutive layer is added. With hand layup, each layer of reinforcing fabric is put in place, rolled out to apply pressure, wet with resin, and then squeegeed to remove any excess. Between each layer of fiberglass, a layer of resin is applied. These are called laminating resins, and they don't completely cure during the laminating process. This ensures that once the hull is finished, a strong primary bond occurs evenly throughout the layers. It eliminates the possibility that layers may cure independently and create weak secondary bonds.

After the final layer of laminate material is applied, an application of finishing resin or finishing gel coat may be applied to the inside surface. This resin includes a surfacing agent that locks out air and allows the resin to set up tack free. Just as hull and deck shapes are proprietary to each builder, so are laminating schedules—the precise what, where, and when of construction.

We've already noted two important layers, resin and gel coat, but these materials add little strength. What gives strength to fiberglass composites are multiple layers of polyester fibers—the "fiber" in fiberglass—and they come in varying types, thicknesses, and weights.

The most common types of fiberglass reinforcement used in boat building are clothlike sheets. **Woven roving** is a rough cloth of polyester fibers woven into an over-and-under, basket-weave pattern. **Biaxial** reinforcement is a more finely woven and expensive cloth that's lighter in weight, and stitched together without an over-and-under pattern. **Triaxial** reinforcement is similar, except that its fibers run in three directions. **Quadaxial** reinforcement, as the name implies, has fibers running in four directions. **Unidirectional** fiberglass is a cloth of long unwoven fibers held together by stitches. Boat builders in recent years have come to realize that hull strength is greatly dependent upon the orientation of fibers in the laminate, and have been making increasing use of directional reinforcement.

Chopped fiberglass is simply a mass of loose fibers or roving mixed with resin. It's sprayed into a mold by a device called a chopper gun, and then rolled out to the desired thickness. In good fishing boats, chopped fiberglass is used sparingly. The problem with chopped fiberglass is that the amount of resin applied is difficult to regulate with a gun, and resin adds weight and thickness but little strength. Chopper guns, however, are sometimes used to apply laminate to non-stress-bearing components, such as the inner liner, engine compartment, stowage compartments, cabin, and the deck. Also,

a layer of chopped fiberglass is sometimes used between woven roving and gel coat to help prevent the rough weave from printing through to the exterior finish.

As noted, each layer of strength-giving fiberglass is accompanied by a layer of resin. In essence, the fiberglass is encapsulated in a resin bath. To maximize laminate strength, excess resin is carefully wiped, squeegeed, or vacuum-bagged before the next layer of fiberglass is applied. Hulls, transoms, and other components that endure great stress have significantly more fiberglass than resin by weight.

In addition to resin and fiberglass, a typical laminate schedule includes layers of **mat**—essentially a cloth made of random polyester fibers pressed flat. Mat is often perforated to enable the resin to seep through for a firmer bond. Sometimes a layer of mat is attached to the back of fiberglass cloth. Mat is used in the laminate process for a number of reasons. In addition to contributing thickness and strength, it prevents the texture of woven roving (which appears as a waffle pattern called **print through** on an otherwise smooth hull) from showing through the gel coat. It also absorbs problematic heat during the curing process, and adjusts to unwanted patterning caused by the varying cure rates of the multiple layers. Altogether, a typical fishing boat will be composed of more than a dozen layers of resin, fiberglass, and mat.

The best fishing boats also use **coring,** which means that a bulky, lightweight material is placed in the laminate schedule between the skin or gel coat and the inner layers of fiberglass and mat. Typical coring materials are polyurethane foam, balsa wood, and thick pieces of mat infused with micro balloons to add bulk but no weight.

In addition to balsa wood, which is typically used in above-water components, other types of wood are often used in laminate schedules to give strength to transoms, decks, engine mounts, and stringers, which are internal support structures. Beyond its strength, wood is an ideal construction material because it maintains its integrity when drilled or hammered into. Fiberglass tends to crack or fracture under such stress.

Stringer systems are important support elements that help the boat maintain its shape and structural integrity, especially under the stress of pounding waves and running at speed. Stringers are typically composed of one or two sets of two-by-fours or two-by-sixes that run along the base of the hull from bow to stern. These stringers are held together by cross members. Layers of resin and fiberglass are typically used to secure stringers in place and seal them from contact with water.

Despite being sealed in laminate, all wood in fiberglass boats is potentially subject to contact with water and eventual rot. This can happen through punctures, normal seepage (fiberglass is actually a semipermeable membrane), and poor repairs or modifications. Boats that spend their entire lives in water generally need wooden **transoms** and stringer systems replaced after about ten years, an

The inner liner drops into the finished hull mold. Its inner sides form the boat's lower deck and bulkheads. In many boats, flotation foam is inserted between the hull and inner liner.

expensive proposition. For this reason, builders continue to search for ways to build boats without wood, such as making transoms with aluminum grids or stringers with molded fiberglass, and replacing stringers altogether by filling the cavity between the hull and the top deck or inner liner with polyurethane foam.

The top deck fits over the hull and inner liner like a cap, enclosing the belowdecks area and forming the main deck.

Polyurethane foam is frequently used in boat building because of a unique property—it's lighter than water and gives the boat positive buoyancy. Polyurethane foam and other buoyant materials are called **flotation foam.** The coast guard requires that boats less than twenty feet long have sufficient flotation to maintain a level attitude, even if the boat is swamped. Flotation material is either laid in hull or component cavities before they're sealed, or it's injected later. In boats longer than twenty feet, adding flotation foam isn't a coast guard requirement, but good builders do include it anyway. Filling structural cavities with flotation foam not only makes a boat buoyant, but adds considerable strength.

When the hull and top deck are cured and

The multiple layers and materials that make up a typical fiberglass boat are bonded together by resins and strengthened by longitudinal and transverse load-bearing supports.

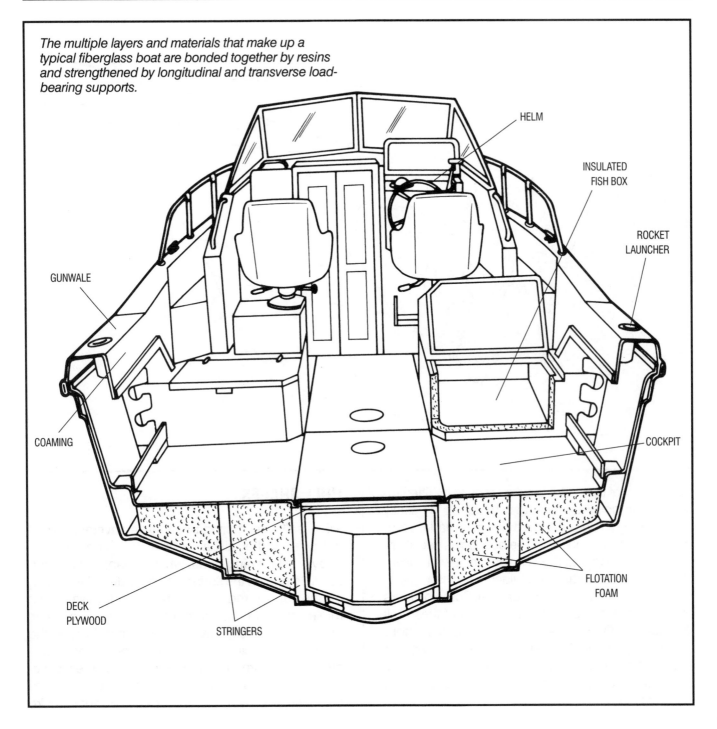

HELM

INSULATED
FISH BOX

ROCKET
LAUNCHER

GUNWALE

COAMING

COCKPIT

FLOTATION
FOAM

DECK
PLYWOOD

STRINGERS

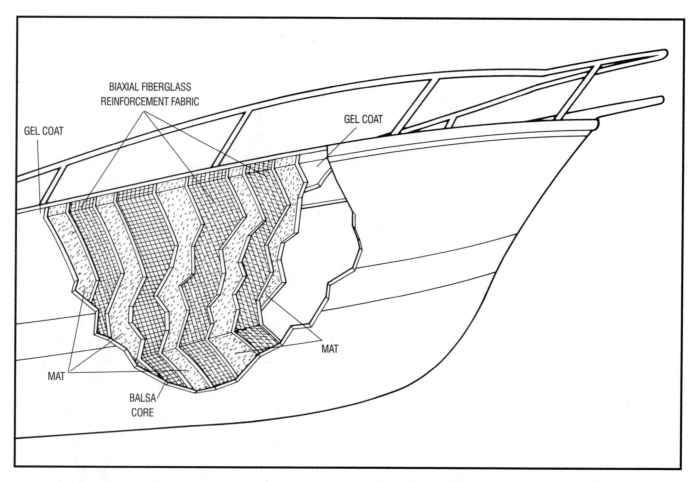

GEL COAT

BIAXIAL FIBERGLASS
REINFORCEMENT FABRIC

GEL COAT

MAT

MAT

BALSA
CORE

popped out of the mold, they're ready to be fitted to-gether. The point at which they're joined is usually disguised by a **rub rail.** How the joint is made is crucial to a boat's soundness. The best boats use stainless-steel screws and then seal the joint with a layer of fiberglass. Less rigorous builders use screws, too, but seal the joint with a bond or glue. Some builders use screws or rivets only, and the best of these will **lag** them with wood. Most offshore and nearshore anglers require joints with stainless-steel screws and a layer of fiberglass. Inshore anglers can get away with a screwed and bonded joint. In either case, using stainles steel is a must.

HULL SHAPES

While saltwater fishing boats have several different hull shapes, they all have one thing in common. They're all **planing hulls,** which means they generate lift to ride on the surface of the water. Since riding on the surface reduces contact with the water to a minimum (and therefore reduces hydrodynamic drag), it's inherently faster than riding through the water or displacing it, which is the operating principle of the common **displacement hull.** In essence, planing hulls have the ability to run over and pass their own bow waves. It takes a lot of power to make

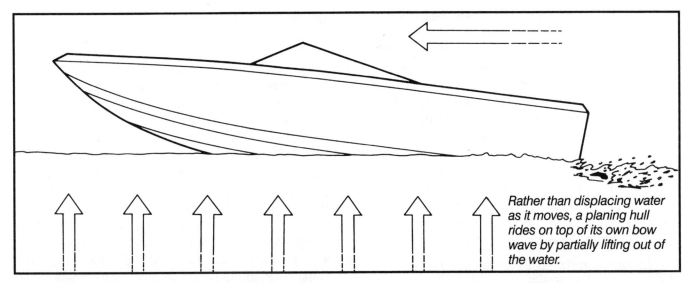

Rather than displacing water as it moves, a planing hull rides on top of its own bow wave by partially lifting out of the water.

a boat rise out of the water, but the benefit is high performance. Slow, steady, and efficient displacement hulls are extremely rare in saltwater fishing boats.

Of the many planing hulls available, by far the most common is the wedge-shaped **V hull.** V hull boats are differentiated by the angle at which the bottom V diverges from the horizontal. Essentially, it is the measurement of the angle that each half of the boat makes from the keel to the waterline. Measured in degrees, it is called **deadrise,** or less commonly, dihedral. A boat with a 0° deadrise would be totally flat. One with an 89° deadrise would be as sharp as the edge of a knife.

Since a planing hull's primary running surface is located at the stern end of the boat, deadrise is measured at the transom. While a few V-bottom boats have a rounded shape known as an oval-V, the typical V hull has a pointed **keel,** a longitudinal line on the hull's bottom that runs down the center of the boat. In addition, it also has two **hard chines,** points where the sides of the hull and the bottom intersect. This angle can be modified to achieve a **reverse chine,** which is a downward dihedral lip, or a hori-

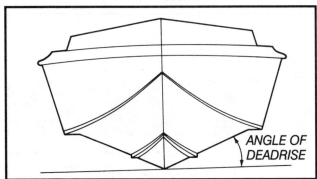

ANGLE OF DEADRISE

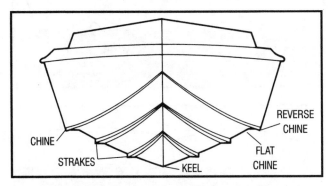

CHINE
STRAKES
KEEL
FLAT CHINE
REVERSE CHINE

Planing hulls are complex structures that feature a number of design components intended to loosen the grip of water on the hull and maintain stability.

9

zontal chine, which is similar to a **strake** but wider. Both help the boat get up on plane, steady it in a beam sea or at rest, and throw spray away from the boat for a dry ride. When a chine has both reverse and horizontal elements, it's called a **double chine.**

V hulls also frequently have two, four, or six strakes, which are sometimes called lifting or running strakes. Strakes are elongated protrusions that run on both sides of the keel, either the entire length from **stem** (the bottom forward portion of the hull) to stern or part way. Combined with the keel, strakes help minimize roll and maintain directional tracking when under way. Combined with hard chines, they help reduce cohesion, the force that holds water to-

Different planing-hull shapes produce varying performance characteristics.

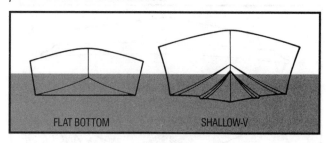
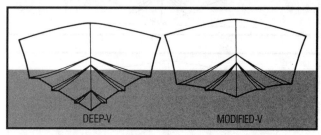
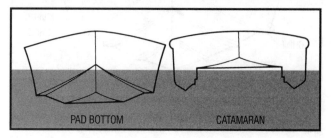

gether, and also throw spray away from the boat. Most strakes have a horizontal bottom at the transom, but as they move forward, they slightly increase their angle of deadrise. This is done to soften the harsh ride produced by having horizontal surfaces near the bow, where they can bang into choppy waves. Adjusting the width of the strake can produce a similar effect.

Developed by Boston-based naval architect C. Raymond Hunt in the late 1950s, the **deep-V** hull is generally one with a deadrise of 18° and higher that's maintained forward at least to amidships. In Hunt's early designs, a 23° deadrise was common. Deep-V hulls knife through waves and therefore provide a so-called soft ride. For this reason, a deep-V with an 18° to 22° deadrise is an ideal choice for an offshore boat. However, since it penetrates water more deeply than a flat hull, it creates more drag and requires bigger engines and more fuel to achieve similar speeds. Deep-V hulls also tend to heel inward when turning and lack side-to-side stability in sloppy seas. Dedicated offshore fishermen put up with these drawbacks in exchange for the ability to run at speed in rough water.

A **modified-V** or **mod-V** hull is generally one with a deadrise between 12° and 17°. It's a compromise between the soft ride of a deep-V and the performance efficiency of a flat bottom. Mod-V boats are generally used for fishing inshore and nearshore waters. Some fishermen, however, take them far offshore when weather and conditions permit.

A **shallow-V** or **flat-V** hull, generally one with a deadrise of less than 12°, is primarily used for inshore fishing. Because of its relatively flat bottom, these boats are ideal for running in shallow water. With drafts less than a foot deep, these rigs skim easily over sandbars and flats where deep-draft boats fear to tread. On the downside, flat-V hulls offer a rough ride in waves and are rarely taken beyond the offshore passes and inlets.

Whatever the angle of deadrise, it's plain that most hulls are wider at the transom than at the bow. This means that the angle of deadrise is not constant throughout, although the term *constant deadrise* is sometimes erroneously applied. In Ray Hunt's early deep-V boats, the deadrise was carried forward quite a bit (as much as two thirds in some boats) before it began to increase sharply toward the bow. Boats like this were said to have constant deadrise to differentiate them from other V-hull concepts of the day. In Hunt's later designs, the deadrise began to increase just forward of the transom. The increase in angle is gradual, at first, but it quickly picks up pace and eventually sharpens to a knifelike 40° at the bow. In addition to altering the deadrise from the transom to the bow, some hulls have different angles of deadrise between each strake. Usually, the sharpest angles of deadrise occur nearest the chines. Hunt also had a hand in popularizing this design, which some boat builders call **variable deadrise** or progressive V.

It's also plain that most hulls have few straight-line sections, and often feature concave and convex segments, especially forward, where a rounded shape is used to add strength and help keep the boat running bow high. Combine this with transom-to-bow variations, strakes, and other bottom components, and the angle of deadrise is sometimes rendered meaningless. This fact may confuse boaters more than help them, but hull design is far from simple. There are many factors that effect performance, and angle of deadrise at the transom is just one of them.

Two V-bottom variations that have a dramatic effect on hull performance are a **pad keel** and a **notched transom.** A pad keel (sometimes called a delta keel) is simply a flat area on the bottom of the hull at the transom. In boats like these, the hull rises out of the water and the boat virtually rides on the small pad. In high-performance boats, the pad can be so long that it will replace the keel. These hulls are called **pad bottoms.** Speed and side-to-side stability are boosted, but so is the roughness of the ride.

A notched transom is a flat cutaway area that recesses the keel line by several inches in a single-engine boat. In dual-engine installations, the notches

Introduced years ago, the twin-hulled catamaran has been slow to win favor among fishermen. However, its impressive rough-water ride is finally winning converts.

or setbacks are widened to encompass both props. The length of the notches are carefully calculated so that the boat still rides mostly on the V, but water flows into the setbacks. This enables the prop and drive unit to be mounted higher out of the water to reduce hydrodynamic drag. Boats with lengthy notches generally have some difficulty getting up on plane. They also perform relatively poorly at much less than full throttle. Both pad keel and notched transom boats have their place in the world of high-performance boating, but are a rarity in saltwater fishing.

One high-performance design that's destined to become more common among offshore fishermen, however, is the **catamaran,** a twin-hulled boat.

Some fishermen may remember that early catamarans experienced difficulty in flexing and handling head seas. It took hull designers some time to work out the best formulas—adjusting bottom configurations and weight placement, and adding more freeboard forward. But the problem has been solved. Today, catamarans have a reputation for providing a good rough-water ride and being especially stable at rest in beam-sea rollers. They earned this reputation by gaining popularity in Australia, New Zealand, and South Africa, locations renowned for their rugged conditions. Several American builders are now making fishing cats, and the trend will likely grow.

POWER OPTIONS

Arriving at the same time as Ray Hunt's deep-V hull was an equally groundbreaking development—the **sterndrive** or I/O engine. This propulsion system, which is an inboard-mounted engine mated to an outboard drive unit, revolutionized offshore boating in the early 1960s for a number of reasons:

1. It offered midsize boats more power than outboards of the time by using big-block automotive engines.
2. It enabled midsize boats to have shallower drafts by mounting the lower gearcase and prop just below the keel line (as opposed to the inboard method of running a prop shaft through the bottom of the hull).
3. Its outdrive could be trimmed up or down to optimize performance, unlike a fixed-shaft inboard.
4. In dual installations, the props could be set to rotate in opposite directions (**counter rotation**) to neutralize the natural starboard bias inherent in outboards.
5. Enclosed in an engine compartment, it was quieter than an outboard and also less prone to give off oily fumes.
6. Because the engine is a **four-cycle** engine (an internal combustion engine that takes four strokes of the piston to accomplish intake of fuel, compression, ignition, and discharge of exhaust), it's less prone than an outboard to foul the spark plugs with oil.

Credit for inventing the ubiquitous sterndrive was given to former Mercury Marine engineer and offshore racer Jim Wynne. However, information has come to light recently that Wynne's friend Charles Strang played a major role in the project. An engineer and executive at Mercury in the 1950s, Strang was caught in an awkward position that divided his loyalties. When Strang and Wynne first proposed building the sterndrive, they wanted to build it at Mercury, but CEO Carl Kiekhaeffer rejected it. Wynne quit the company, but Strang, Kiekhaeffer's second in command, stayed. Wynne eventually persuaded the Swedish company Volvo Penta to build the new engine, but operational and manufacturing problems still needed to be solved. Wynne needed help, and he got it from his old pal Strang, an M.I.T. graduate. Strang helped on the condition that Wynne keep his role a secret. And so it was for thirty years, even though Strang left Mercury himself and eventually became chief executive officer of Outboard Marine Company (OMC), Mercury's main rival.

Despite the early advantages of sterndrives, **outboard engines**—transom-mounted internal-combustion gas engines that use **two cycles** (or two strokes) of the piston to accomplish intake, compression, ignition, and exhaust—soon gained favor by building larger power plants, and adding counter rotation and oil injection. Once these improvements were made, the outboard, popularized by Ole Evinrude after the turn of the century, began to capitalize on a natural advantage of its own:

Cutaway transoms and splash wells are the hallmark of the typical outboard boat. To prevent following seas from swamping the boat, many are equipped with flip-up splash boards.

Bolt-on outboard brackets were developed not only to improve boat performance by extending the length of the hull, but to enable builders to use full, protective transoms.

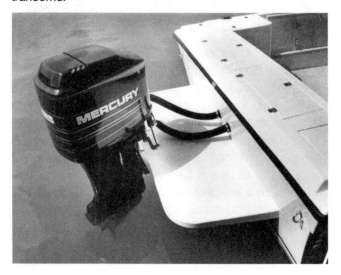

By integrating the outboard bracket into the hull, boat builders maximize the bracket's performance-enhancing potential and eliminate the trial-and-error process of installing a bolt-on component.

the fact that it occupies no onboard space.

Sterndrives not only occupy onboard space (as do inboards), but they do so in the critical cockpit area right at the transom. This is the area where most anglers fight fish, and a bulky engine box can be a serious impediment. For this reason, sterndrives have become relatively uncommon in serious fishing boats.

Outboards, on the other hand, are a popular power option for offshore fishermen, especially in recent years. In addition to freeing up deck space, outboards are lighter than sterndrive or inboard engines, easier to access for maintenance, and they're capable of being mounted on extender brackets and jack plates to improve boat performance.

In recent years, **outboard brackets,** two- to three-foot fiberglass extender pieces added to the transom at the waterline, have become increasingly popular performance options on small and midsize boats. Outboards, either in single or dual installations, are mounted on these brackets instead of on the transom. The effect is to move the props aft into ideal water flow and to increase the hull's length, which improves the boat's performance. This also moves the outboard out of the way to increase fish-fighting space and reduce operating noise and fumes. Many boat builders now offer outboard brackets as standard equipment (some are built right into the mold) or as an option.

Jack plates are another device installed between the transom and the outboard to improve performance. A jack plate enables a boater to move the entire outboard engine vertically up or down. This is independent from the familiar adjustment called **trim,** which refers to swinging the prop and lower gearcase up or down in an arc. Jack plates can be either manual or hydraulic. With a manual jack plate, the outboard is hoisted into one of several positions and then locked in place. With a hydraulic jack plate, boaters press a button to adjust engine height, even while under way. Jack plates were originally devised to help high-performance boaters reduce drag by raising their lower gearcases as far out of the water as possible. Inshore fishermen use them to reduce draft for running in shallow waters.

Despite some natural advantages, outboards weren't always considered a saltwater fisherman's friend. As recently as the early 1980s, outboards were plagued by two major problems: frequent spark-plug fouling, due to a crude 50:1 gas/oil delivery system; and swift corrosion. The addition of automatic oil-injection and, in recent years, electronic engine-management systems, solved most of the problems related to fouling and reliability. To cope with saltwater corrosion, manufacturers added a high percentage of stainless-steel parts, high-grade alloys, and effective anticorrosion coatings and paints. Today, a properly cared-for outboard should last as long as a sterndrive or inboard engine.

Neither sterndrive nor outboard engines were used on Hemingway's *Pilar.* During the early and mid-part of this century, fishermen exclusively used

inboards, center-mounted, internal-combustion, four-cycle engines that run a prop shaft through the bottom of the hull. Today, inboard engines, either in single or dual installations, still have an exclusive domain. They are typically used in midsize or larger boats. While inboard engines can burn gas, most of those used in fishing boats burn diesel fuel. Although **diesel engines** are four-cycle internal-combustion engines, they differ from gas engines by burning small amounts of low-combustion fuel at relatively low revolutions per minute (rpm). They are able to do this by forcing the fuel to undergo tremendous compression pressures in the cylinder to amplify the force of ignition.

Since heavy V-shaped hulls must run at mid- to high-throttle settings to get up on plane, big-boat fishermen favor diesel engines because they operate at slower rpm and burn measurably less fuel. However, diesels aren't for everyone. Two big reasons why are initial cost and weight, both of which are frequently double that for a comparable gas engine. In a large, high-dollar fishing boat, these factors are partly neutralized by the rig's overall scale. Since everything else is bigger, the cost and weight of the engine seem to be in line. In the long run, these boats will achieve measurable savings by burning less fuel.

But this is not automatically the case with mid- and small-boat fishermen. Although small diesel engines are becoming more popular in the United States and have been common in Europe for decades, the high initial price is prohibitive when calculated as a percentage of the overall boat. It means that savings won't start to materialize until five or more years of heavy use. Also, diesel engines are relatively more expensive to maintain and repair. So, for midsize and small-boat fishermen, it's a good idea to work out the math before buying a diesel engine.

CHAPTER 2

VERSATILE CENTER CONSOLES

Today, center-console boats are the most versatile boats in fishing, but it wasn't always that way. Up to the 1960s, they were primarily used for inshore fishing or as tenders for larger vessels. However, two innovations changed everything: unsinkable foam flotation and V-bottom hulls. The addition of these elements complemented certain natural advantages of center consoles, and it eventually made them the most popular fishing boats on the water.

While it's hard to pin down which boat builder mated flotation foam to a center-console boat, it's easy to name the builder that became famous for it: Boston Whaler. In the early 1960s, the company earned a national reputation for building unsinkable boats, due in large part to a famous photo, which showed the company president sitting in a boat that had been cut into three pieces. What the photo illustrated was that structural cavities within the boat were filled with closed-cell foam flotation. These cavities were created by joining a top deck to a hull, a

Considered the most versatile of fishing rigs, center-console boats range from small, inshore flat bottoms to large, offshore deep-V hulls. This is a midsize model heading out beyond the jetty.

sophisticated boat-building technique that was quickly supplanting the use of a simple one-piece mold. The flotation foam was either hand-laid or injected into the spaces between the two components. This not only made boats more buoyant, but gave them rock-solid stiffness, a highly desirable characteristic in an era when many fiberglass hulls displayed power-robbing flex. The famous Whaler photo appeared in numerous publications, including *Life* magazine.

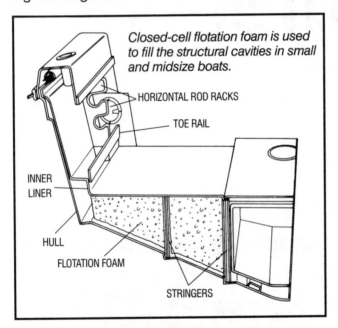

Closed-cell flotation foam is used to fill the structural cavities in small and midsize boats.

HORIZONTAL ROD RACKS

TOE RAIL

INNER LINER

HULL

FLOTATION FOAM

STRINGERS

Armed with a reputation for building solid and unsinkable center consoles, Whaler became increasingly popular with fishermen who not only used them to stalk inshore bays, but took them beyond the jetties to fish nearshore waters when weather permitted. However, despite the soundness of their hulls, fishermen soon found that Whaler's distinctive **tri-hull** or cathedral-hull design was far from ideal in rough water. (A tri-hull or a cathedral hull is a planing hull characterized by a blunt bow and three side-by-side, V-shaped bottom components.) While tri-hull

bottoms delivered fine all-around performance on flat water, they provided a hard, wet ride in a wind-blown chop of just a foot or two. In bigger seas, the ride became progressively worse.

The solution to the small-boat, rough-water problem was a new bottom design—the deep-V hull, which knifed through chop and rollers comfortably and at speed. This design, developed by Boston-based naval architect Raymond Hunt, appeared in the late 1950s on yacht tenders and racing boats. Despite the geographical proximity between Hunt and Whaler, the first builder that fully exploited the

Although small, this center-console boat features perimeter walkability and is well outfitted with a T-top, leaning post, and an overhead electronics box.

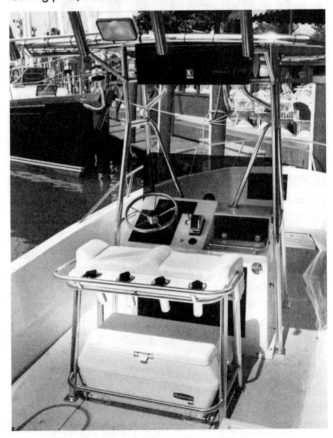

advantages of the deep-V on center-console boats was based in Miami.

As it is with the early development of foam flotation, it's a little difficult to pin down exactly which company was the first to join a deep-V hull to a center-console deck, but there's no doubt that Aquasport is the company that became famous for it. Once these components were mated—center-console layout, positive flotation, deep-V and mod-V hulls—the genie was let out of the bottle. In short order, Aquasport, Mako, Whaler, and many others helped make the center-console design the most ubiquitous fishing boat on the water.

In addition to excellent rough-water performance and fish-fighting features, a large part of a center console's appeal is simplicity and affordability. Since most center consoles range from sixteen feet to twenty-four feet long, sticker prices fall within reach of the average American budget. Equally important, operating costs are fairly low because the boats can use small engines and be stored on trailers. As a result of an overall keep-it-simple philosophy, most center consoles are built without labor-intensive teak trim and require little more sprucing up than a thorough wash down from a freshwater hose.

Beyond cost, versatility is another appealing trait. In good conditions, fishermen can take V-bottom center consoles many miles offshore for deep-water trolling or fishing over wrecks; in less-than-ideal weather, they can stay near shore; in poor conditions, they can stay inside the jetties and cast on the flats. Depending on the elements, virtually the entire world of saltwater fishing is open to center-console boats.

THE CENTER CONSOLE

No matter how large or small, all **center-console boats** have several things in common: a planing V

hull; foam flotation; and a gas engine, typically an outboard but not always. But there's a fourth component that center consoles also possess: a raised control unit mounted amidships. This unit can be either integrated into the deck mold or bolted on as a separate component. Some of these units are generously outfitted with features. Some are little more than a bare fiberglass box. But at a minimum, all of these units have a dash panel fitted with instruments and gauges, plus a helm station equipped with operational controls. These units are called center consoles.

The primary function of a center console is to provide the captain with a remote station for driving the boat. Prior to the development of center consoles, small boats basically had two options (still common today): **tiller-handle** controls (which are seen frequently on small **skiffs**) and side-mounted control units affixed to the starboard gunwale (called **side consoles**).

While tiller-handle outboards are fine on relatively protected rivers and lakes, saltwater fishermen deal with severe windblown chop and ocean rollers. In conditions like these, the driver's hands not only operate the controls, but also help maintain balance and support. Saltwater fishermen quickly discovered the awkward sitting and hand positions required to operate the tiller handle made driving difficult in moderate and heavy seas. They also discovered that this configuration shifts a significant portion of weight to the stern. A low, heavy stern matched with a high, light bow is less than ideal in a small, pitching boat.

Uneven boat balance is also the reason that single side-console layouts (less costly alternatives to installing dual consoles) are uncommon in saltwater boats. The intended purpose of mounting a single console on the side of a boat is to help counter the twisting motion (**torque**) produced by the prop. Since props rotate in a counterclockwise direction, boats at speed tend to lean to port. To compensate, builders shift weight to the opposite side.

But prop torque, which only comes into play at speed, is just one of many forces a saltwater fisherman contends with. Off plane and offshore—for trolling or jigging or casting at structure—a starboard-weighted boat will be subject to uncomfortable pitching and heeling. Center-weighted boats have a clear advantage in conditions like these.

There's also a practical reason for moving the console away from the starboard **gunwale**: freedom of movement. By positioning the console in the center, fishermen are able to move completely around the perimeter of the boat without encountering a fixed obstacle. Movement of 360° is important during the heat of battle when every move counts, especially for bottom fishermen who frequently get multiple hookups. It also comes in handy during docking, when tying up requires easy access fore and aft.

Beyond these architectural considerations, the center console is an ideal unit for mounting important fishing and operational features. These include instruments and gauges typically found on a nonglare dash panel: throttle, trim switch, trim-tab controls, speedometer, tachometer, volt meter, fuel gauge, trim gauge, engine-water temperature gauge, warning lights, ignition switch, and emergency shutoff switch. It also includes switches for the bilge pump, blower, navigation lights, courtesy lights, live-well aerator, live-well pump, horn, and other accessories. Boats with engine trim and trim tabs have indicator gauges for each system.

Aside from the dash panel, the flat top of the console is a good surface for mounting important electronic instruments (discussed in detail in Chapter 6), such as: a loran-C receiver, VHF radio, compass, GPS receiver, sonar depth-sounder/fish-finder, radar, radio/cassette player, and others.

On large, well-designed center consoles, lockable compartments are used as an electronics box (for mounting one or more of the electronic units mentioned above) or for stowage of maps, binoculars, flashlight, flares, air horn, fire extinguisher, batteries, and other safety gear. Some center consoles also have side storage compartments, although most of these are simply secondary hatches that provide access to a large under-console space. Some, however, may feature built-in tackle boxes with multiple trays, and less frequently, a **tackle rigging station** with a cutting board and room to spread out hooks, leader, sinkers, and so forth.

Other features frequently found on well-designed center consoles are: windscreens, for protection against rain and spray; grab handles, to offer passengers a secure handhold; toe rails, for a place to hook your feet in rough conditions; footrests, ei-

These vertical rod holders are fixed to a T-top above the helm area. Although typically used for rod storage, they can also be used as rod mounts for kite flying or multibait trolling patterns.

ther fixed or adjustable; antennae for VHF radio, GPS, loran-C, and so forth; vertical rod holders (often called **rocket launchers**) for standing storage of multiple rods and reels; a forward-facing padded seat, which usually sits atop a cooler or stowage compartment in front of the console; and built-in drink holders for juice, soft drinks, or water. In some large boats, the center console lifts up or has an opening hatch to reveal a belowdecks compartment used as a marine head or, less frequently, an engine compartment for an inboard engine.

Even the smallest consoles provide ideal mounting platforms for protective canvas tops. The sim-

plest of these are called **Bimini tops,** which are mounted on tubular aluminum or stainless-steel supports, typically fixed to the gunwales and pulled taut by tie-down straps. Welded-aluminum **towers** are sturdy, weight-bearing structures that are not only used for overhead protection, but for mounting important equipment and accessories. Since they are anchored to either the deck sole, the console, or a combination of both, these towers have the additional advantage of allowing freedom of movement around the console without the problem of running into tubes or tie-down straps. Both structures can be fitted with protective front and

A classic welded-aluminum T-top fitted with canvas to protect the helm area from sun and rain. It also has rocket launchers, antennae mounts, and an overhead electronics box.

side **curtains** to help keep out wind, rain, and spray. These curtains are typically zippered into place and made of canvas and clear plastic.

The simplest type of aluminum tower is called a **T-top.** In addition to overhead protection, the sturdy T-top is an ideal structure for mounting antennae, vertical rod holders, overhead electronics lockers, cockpit lights, and floodlights. Another accessory frequently mounted on towers are **outriggers,** which are tall aluminum poles on either side of the boat typically fitted with spreaders and tension cables. Their purpose is to keep lines from multiple rods tangle-free, and lures and bait from skipping on top of the water as they often do when simply run from a low, gunwale-mounted, flexible rod.

A popular variation of the T-top is known as a **hard top,** which uses a rectangle of hard fiberglass overhead instead of canvas. Weight-sensitive fishermen use hard tops only for adding overhead plat-

forms, because the heavy components can contribute to a boat's tendency to rock and roll. In small center consoles, light canvas is the best choice for keeping out sun and rain.

A bigger, more complex version of the hard top is a tower with a **spotting platform** and raised **belly rails.** This type of tower is used to seek out gamefish or signs of where they might be located. Height is a distinct advantage when scanning for fish.

On large boats, spotting platforms are frequently rigged with a second helm station with complete operational controls. Towers like these shift a boat's center of gravity significantly upward, and few V-bottom center-console boats under twenty-five feet in length have the beam and heft to carry them. It generally takes a twenty-five-foot-long center-console boat to carry a high-profile, dual-helm tower. To carry a three-story **tuna tower** or marlin tower, the boat should be in the thirty-foot range and larger.

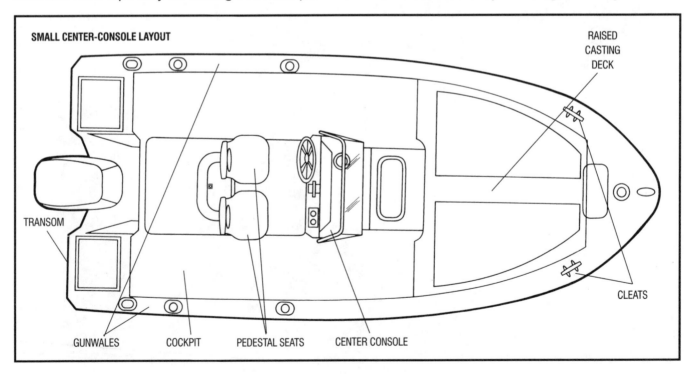

SMALL CENTER-CONSOLE LAYOUT

RAISED CASTING DECK

TRANSOM

CLEATS

GUNWALES   COCKPIT   PEDESTAL SEATS   CENTER CONSOLE

SMALL CENTER CONSOLES

Originally designed as modest-sized, inshore boats, center consoles today can be large, offshore craft. The most popular models, however, are still in the seventeen-foot to twenty-foot range. Beams on boats of this size run from six feet six inches to eight feet six inches. Gross weight, including engine and all accessories, runs from fifteen hundred pounds to three thousand pounds. Drafts can be anywhere from seven inches to two feet six inches.

Most of the boats in this category generally have modified-V and shallow-V hulls, although a fair number have deep-Vs. Fuel capacity starts at thirty gallons and runs up to one hundred. Well-designed boats in this category have self-bailing cockpits and live wells, plus compartments that drain over the side, as opposed to flooding the bilge. Prices run the gamut from seven thousand dollars, for a stripped-down hull, to twenty thousand, for a fully outfitted rig.

As noted, the power of choice for center consoles is the outboard motor with hydraulic-assisted steering and a stainless-steel prop. For boats less than twenty feet long, this means a single outboard from 90 horsepower to 225 horsepower. With either size engine, these light craft will have enough power to run at high-performance speeds (typically around 50 mph), which is one of their chief attributes.

Boats of twenty feet or less in length are probably the closest thing on the market to a prototypical center console. The smallest of these have a flat cockpit sole or deck; however, many have a raised bow area that's useful for casting. All deck and walking areas have **nonskid surfaces,** either geometric patterns cut into the mold or a gel-coat finish with a sandlike texture. Marine carpeting is rarely seen in the deck area of a true center-console boat, or any saltwater fishing boat.

Foredeck and aft cockpit areas are generally about equal, since the console is virtually centered. Depending on the beam of the boat, there will be a one- to two-foot walking space between the console and the side bulkhead. Cockpit depth (measured from the deck to the top of the gunwale) is approximately two feet, or just above the knees, and overall, boats in this category have a relatively low-to-the-water profile.

Most center consoles in this range come with dual adjustable chairs, which can be swiveled and moved backward for use as fish-fighting chairs. At speed,

A sure sign of quality, hawse pipes that lead to side-hull cleats eliminate chaffing of the gunwale by dock lines and snag points for fishing line.

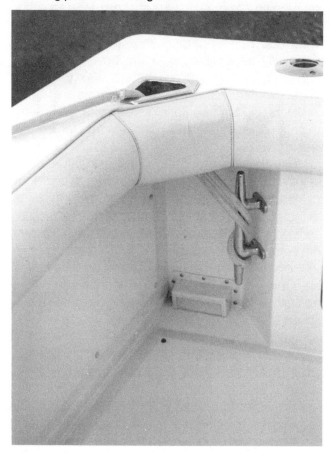

they can also be moved out of the way to allow driver and passenger to ride standing up, the method of choice when the water gets rough. Often a cooler or a portable live well is located below or aft of the swivel chairs, and fixed in place with shock cords.

As mentioned, boats of this size can be purchased inexpensively with little more than a bare deck, control console, and seats. However, most fishermen and boat builders today outfit them with a large package of equipment and accessories. Staring at the transom, this can include a removable/folding splashboard; two small compartments for general stowage or batteries; a hatch-lid cutting board; a navigation-light mount; and a raw-water wash-down hose. Also at the transom, located either in an aft storage box or below a deck hatch, are batteries and **bilge** pumps. Since these boats may potentially take waves over the bow or transom, high-capacity bilge pumps in the 1,000-gph range are recommended. While swim platforms are handy for divers and family entertaining, they're rarely seen on serious fishing rigs. The same is true for ski-tow eyes.

Along the sides of the boat, typical features can include bolster pads on the **coaming;** two to four rocket launchers recessed into the gunwales; cleats on the gunwale (located forward and away from fishing lines on well-built boats); recessed **hawse pipes** that lead to cleats mounted away from fishing lines on the side bulkhead; horizontal rod holders below the gunwales; and mounts for antennae and Bimini tops. In the forward section, there is generally a railing on the gunwale, a bow anchor chock, a bow navigation light, and an anchor locker.

Stowage compartments in boats of this size are somewhat limited. They're usually confined to small boxes at the transom; space beneath the console; coolers either fore or aft of the console (frequently portable units attached to the deck with shock cords); and two or three compartments beneath the forward deck, at least one of which is for dry storage and one designated as an insulated fish box. In addition, some boats will have attachment points in front of the console to mount portable tackle boxes with shock cords.

MIDSIZE CENTER CONSOLES

Midsize center consoles, roughly twenty feet to twenty-four feet long, don't necessarily have to run to shore when storm clouds gather. Properly equipped with electronics and safety gear, they can handle surprisingly nasty weather and make fairly long offshore runs. Generally, they will have beams that run from seven feet six inches to eight feet six inches. Gross weight, including engine and accessories, can be two thousand pounds to four thousand pounds. Drafts run anywhere from seven inches to two feet six inches.

Most of the boats in this category have modified-V and deep-V hulls. Shallow-Vs are rare. Fuel capacity starts at fifty gallons and runs to one hundred fifty gallons. Prices start at a lean-and-mean fifteen thousand dollars and run to thirty thousand for full outfitting.

Naturally, midsize center consoles can be equipped with most of the features listed for their smaller cousins and quite a few more. One of the first things added is a second outboard motor. Most boats in this category are rated to run from 200 to 300 horsepower. Until recently, the typical fisherman would hang a pair of matching 135-horse or 150-horse outboards on his transom, depending on the boat's maximum power rating. Even though individual outboards can deliver up to 300 horsepower, many fishermen opted for a twin-outboard setup to provide backup power in case one engine failed. Properly cared-for modern outboards are far more reliable than their older counterparts, but the twin-

Above: Twin-engine outboard installations are favored by midsize and large center consoles, preferably with a bracket and full transom.
Right: The larger the center console, the more instruments, gauges, electronics equipment, controls, and storage compartments can be fitted into the helm area.

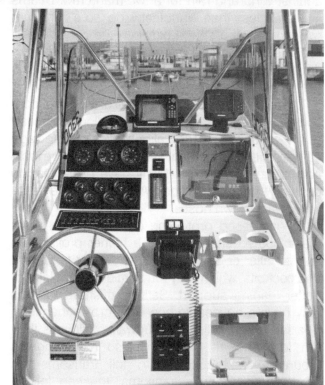

engine tradition still prevails. This is so even though twin engines are heavier, burn more fuel, and are more maintenance intensive than an equivalent single engine. To help improve running characteristics, heavier center consoles frequently use outboard brackets.

In recent years, there has been some movement toward a setup with a large, main engine and a small **kicker motor.** The main engine is used for typical operational situations, especially running on plane. The kicker, which is mounted to the side of the main motor, is used for slow trolling, although it can be used as a backup in an emergency.

Virtually all boats of this size are equipped with hydraulically controlled **trim tabs,** which are twin steel or fiberglass planes or plates located at the bottom of the transom. Trim tabs move up and down, both individually and in unison, and alter the flow of water beneath the hull. In the down position, the tabs raise the stern and lower the bow. In the up position, they have the opposite effect. Controlled by buttons on the dash, trim tabs help heavy or aft-weighted boats get on plane. In beam or quartering seas, they help boats run level. In the down position, the port-side tab helps level boats when wind and waves are coming from starboard. The starboard-side tab, in the down position, has the opposite effect.

Boats in the twenty-foot to twenty-four-foot class have much more complex center-console units than smaller boats. The consoles are generally taller (counting a topside lockable compartment and a windscreen) and provide standing protection against wind and rain for a two-man crew. Beams are rarely less than eight feet wide, so a minimum two-foot walking space between the console and the side bulkheads is fairly standard. However, this doesn't mean deck space is copious. As the boats get larger, so do the consoles.

The forward areas on virtually all of the larger consoles have bench seats with padding located ahead of the windscreen. They also have large stowage compartments underneath. Most have topside lockable electronics boxes. Many have built-in tackle boxes with rigging stations. A few may have fresh-water wash-down hoses.

For increased protection during offshore runs, these boats generally sport a higher profile than their smaller cousins, and have deeper freeboard and cockpits, which may run to mid-thigh height for better leaning support. Serious offshore runners may have a noticeable bow-high profile thanks to a raised **sheer,** a line the gunwales follow as they run fore and aft. They will also have engines mounted on brackets with full transoms, as opposed to cutaway transoms, to keep follow-

A typical leaning post with grab rails, rocket launchers, and a deck-mounted cooler.

ing seas from flooding the cockpit.

While many of these boats sport dual adjustable chairs, a large number are fitted with **leaning posts,** which are wide padded bolsters installed in place of individual seats. The advantage of the leaning post is that it conforms to the way most fishermen drive their boats—standing up—and it forms a good structure to mount other accessories, such as rocket launchers, grab rails, and (in the back) a stowage box or rigging station. The open space beneath the leaning post is often filled by a cooler or live well, either portable or built-in.

Live wells on boats like these can be found on the

transom or in the deck. Tackle rigging stations and wash-down hoses are typically found at the transom. Boats of this size sometimes carry gunwale-mounted **downriggers,** manual or electronic rod-and-reel units used for deep-water trolling. Other accessories frequently seen on these boats include a T-top with a spotting tower, a bow-mounted fighting chair, and a bow pulpit with anchor hardware.

Stowage compartments on boats of this size can include medium-to-large transom boxes; space beneath the console (occasionally large enough for a marine head); two or three large compartments below the foredeck; and sometimes an aft storage box or two below the cockpit. For the comfort of crew and family members, raised storage boxes are sometimes fitted with snap-on pads to create seats.

LARGE CENTER CONSOLES

With center-console boats now running twenty-five feet to thirty-five feet in length, builders are now deal-ing with an animal different from the prototypical center console. Small center consoles are generally thought of as affordable, go-anywhere boats. Large center consoles are dedicated offshore fishing machines.

Boats in this class never run less than eight feet wide. Most run from eight feet six inches (still easily trailerable) to nine feet six inches in width (which requires special road permits). An elite few break the beamy eleven foot barrier. Gross weight runs from three thousand pounds to about seven thousand pounds. Drafts run from one to three feet.

Deep-V bottoms are the norm in this bluewater category, but a fair number will sport modified-V hulls. Fuel capacity can be less than one hundred gallons and more than two hundred gallons. Prices start in the neighborhood of thirty thousand dollars for a basic package and run all the way up to six figures for a top-of-the-line warrior.

Power of choice in this class is twin outboards. However, with maximum power ratings beginning at 300 horsepower and running to 600 horsepower,

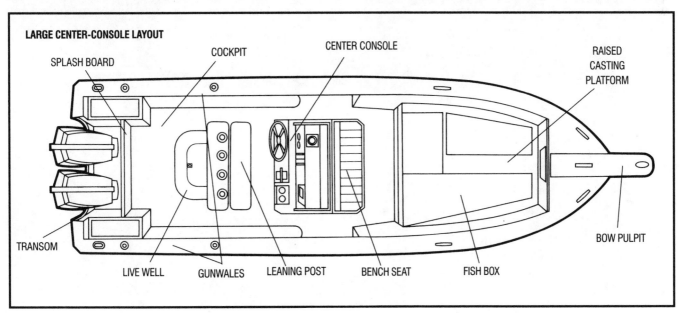

LARGE CENTER-CONSOLE LAYOUT

SPLASH BOARD
COCKPIT
CENTER CONSOLE
RAISED CASTING PLATFORM
TRANSOM
BOW PULPIT
LIVE WELL
GUNWALES
LEANING POST
BENCH SEAT
FISH BOX

there are several options. As already noted, most fishermen typically choose twin 150-horse to 300-horse outboards (frequently with a bracket), because this installation takes up the least onboard space. However, a minority takes advantage of the boat's bigger space and heft to install a large gas or diesel inboard engine, located beneath the console, or a sterndrive engine, which is located in a compartment at the transom. No marine power package burns fuel as copiously as twin, high-rpm outboards, so relatively low-rpm inboard or sterndrive engines are options that can conserve fuel. On the downside, inboards require a rudder-and-prop assembly that sharply increases draft, while sterndrives place a fixed obstruction in the prime fish-fighting area of the cockpit.

This center console is a hybrid boat that sports a small cuddy compartment in the bow.

Welded-aluminum tops are weight-bearing structures that can accommodate overhead electronics boxes. These boxes enable fishermen to unclutter the dash area and protect sensitive instruments.

Although these boats are rated for high-horsepower engines, top speeds are lower for big center consoles, because of their beamier and heavier hulls. Typically, large center consoles run in the 30-mph to 40-mph range. A fair number will push mid-to-high 40s. Only a few will hit 50 mph or more.

While layouts in these boats are roughly similar to their smaller cousins, the larger platforms give builders a few more options to work with. One of these is to alter the amidships location of the console aft a few feet to create more space in the bow and to shift weight to the stern for better planing performance. A few builders take this approach a step further. After moving the console, they put a modest **cuddy cabin** in the bow with spartan accommodations that typically include berths, a minimal galley, and a head.

Since these boats are designed for long, offshore trips, they typically feature deep, protective cockpits and freeboard, and sheers that angle upward toward the bow. Some builders take the raised sheer to a radical level by splitting it amidships. In essence, boats with **split sheers** have two different sheer lines, fore and aft. This allows the boat to have a low cockpit for reaching over the side to handle lines, bait, and fish. It also allows the forward section to have a high freeboard where it's needed in heavy seas. To help offshore safety, twin automatic bilge pumps with total capacities of 2000 gph to 3000 gph are virtually standard equipment.

All the accessories and equipment already mentioned in connection with small center consoles can be found on larger boats. In fact, while many of these are options on small center consoles, they're virtually standard equipment on large ones. However, there are some distinctive features found only on large craft, such as: radar arches for mounting radar antennae, rocket launchers, outriggers, and more; dual-control towers three stories high; full-canvas enclosures, which cover both the console

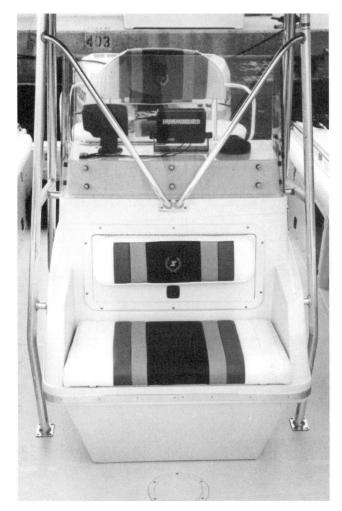

The bench seat forward of the center console not only adds to multipassenger seating capacity, but typically serves as the lid of a cooler

and the bow; transom doors, which ease the task of hauling in fish; fore or aft fighting chairs (sometimes both); rocket launchers in the transom for kite fishing; autopilot, for long-range runs; and whatever else money can buy.

While large center consoles may not have the comfort and luxury of big cabin boats, they have everything else a serious fisherman needs in spades.

CHAPTER 3

MIDSIZE WALKAROUNDS AND CUDDY CABINS

The birth of modern offshore sportfishing should probably be dated to the mid 1970s, a time when the popular center console was joined by the equally popular **walkaround**—a shortened name for a walkaround cabin boat. This was an era when a number of technical and cultural elements fell into place: advanced fiberglass construction, powerful outboard motors, sport-specific design, booming desire, and sticker prices that were within reach of many average Americans.

One of the first builders to capitalize on this happy convergence, especially in the area of walkarounds, was Grady-White, a North Carolina company with a regional following. Begun in the late 1950s, Grady-White was originally known for building plywood lapstrake skiffs with flared Carolina bows. Interestingly, Grady-White built these well-received wooden classics long after most companies had converted to fiberglass.

However, by the early 1970s, Grady-White had converted, too, and in 1975, it married a fiberglass walkaround deck to a medium-size outboard-powered hull. This development and the emerging forces of the times helped move Grady-White from strictly regional popularity to a much broader market. Today, Grady-White is one of the largest saltwater fishing boat builders in the country.

Grady-White didn't actually invent the walkaround concept, just as Boston Whaler and Aquasport didn't actually invent the modern center console. What the North Carolina–based builder did was bring together various existing marine elements, and mate them in a way that performed extremely well. For example, the idea of reducing the size of the cuddy cabin in proportion to the length and width of the hull was not exactly new at the time; neither was building side decks and a forward deck at the cockpit level to improve fore-and-aft walking and fishing around the perimeter of the boat. These concepts probably derive from small New England lobster

Slow trolling through Miami's Government Cut, this walkaround tests the waters for fish before heading offshore.

boats, hard-cabin sportfishermen, or pilothouse boats.

Other elements, too, were equally derivative: fiberglass construction, planing V hull, inner liner, stringer system, foam flotation, outboard power, and relatively low sheer line, especially aft. But the achievement is in pulling the elements together and making them work as a unified whole. Since the mid 1970s, the walkaround concept has been copied and modified until it has become a classic. Today, walkarounds are built by more than two dozen companies, and there's little doubt that regional lap-strake-skiff builder Grady-White surfed the wave of the walkaround's success to create a national following.

As the second most common fishing boat on saltwater after the center console, the walkaround shares several fundamental characteristics with its popular cousin. Chief among these is versatility. The walkaround design works as well on eighteen-foot hulls as it does on hulls longer than thirty-five feet.

The typical walkaround features an open cockpit that leads to a helm area on the same deck. Perimeter decks protected by raised gunwales run around the small cuddy to a flat foredeck.

True, the cabins are rarely used for genuine overnighting, especially on boats less than twenty-five feet long, but they provide good protection from spray at the helm, a place to relax when the weather becomes overbearing, and security for keeping stowage dry and equipment safe.

Other shared characteristics are affordability, especially in the small eighteen-foot to twenty-four-foot class, and low maintenance, since they are typically built without teak flourishes and with a minimum of cabin accoutrement. Also, like center consoles, even the smallest walkarounds can run many miles offshore in good conditions, and fish in the same neighborhood as the big boys. Flotation foam is rarely required in walkarounds, since the coast guard only requires it in boats less than twenty feet long, but the best walkarounds inject it between the hull and inner liner to add stiffness and strength.

Unique to walkarounds is a sense of comfort that is decidedly missing from more spartan center consoles. The walkaround design offers builders great opportunities to integrate features not possible on the typical center console, and to install padded seating for more than a two-man crew. Creature comforts like these are increasingly important as fishing boat selection becomes more of a family-influenced decision.

THE WALKAROUND

The name *walkaround* derives from the craft's layout, which allows fishermen to walk and fish easily around the boat's outer perimeter. Of course, the center console accomplishes this feat, too, but it does so by eliminating virtually all deck structure. The walkaround is a more complex design.

To achieve 360° walking decks or catwalks, the walkaround establishes a deck level on either side of the cabin and extends it forward all the way to the bow. Cuddy-cabin boats, on the other hand, differ by forcing fishermen to walk on the gunwales or over the deckhouse. This is possible when going forward to work the anchor, but not practical when fighting a fish. Additionally, the foredecks on cuddy cabins are simply the contoured tops of the cabins themselves, and not a dedicated deck area.

Walkarounds, on the other hand, take a completely different approach by building dedicated **side decks** (frequently more than six inches wide) for easy access around the sides of the cabin. The differences between true side decks (as on walk-

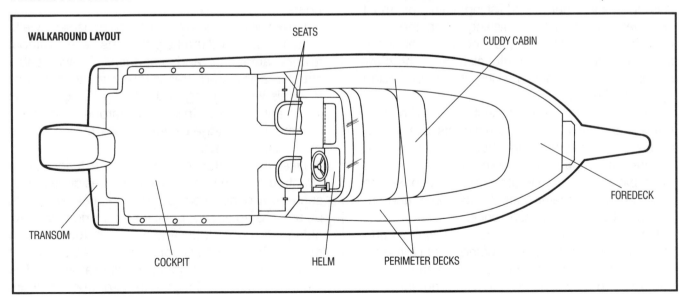

WALKAROUND LAYOUT

SEATS · CUDDY CABIN · FOREDECK · PERIMETER DECKS · HELM · COCKPIT · TRANSOM

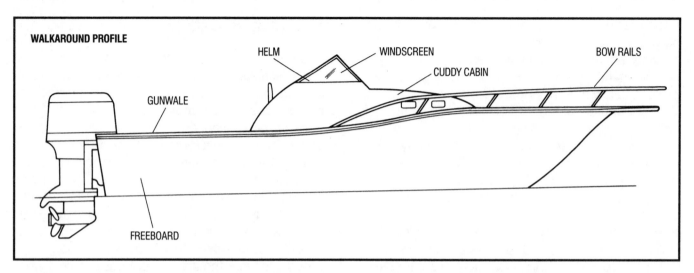

WALKAROUND PROFILE

HELM   WINDSCREEN   BOW RAILS

CUDDY CABIN

GUNWALE

FREEBOARD

arounds) and walkable gunwales (as on cuddy-cabin boats) are threefold: Side decks have nonskid surfaces; they are protected by raised hull sides; and their level is within a step or two of the level of the cockpit. These same principles extend to the foredeck, which together with the side decks and aft cockpit creates a unified walking perimeter.

The advantage of having 360° walking capability is important in a number of fishing scenarios, most especially during bottom fishing when the crew may be large and multiple hookups frequently occur. The walkable perimeter also helps the crew perform anchoring and docking chores by easing access to the bow.

A second definitive component of the walkaround is the cuddy cabin. On true cabin boats, every effort is made by designers and builders to maximize interior cabin space. On walkarounds, the size of the cabin is secondary to other considerations—the width of the perimeter deck, for example, and enlargement of the fish-fighting cockpit.

Consequently, cuddys in the small walkaround classes rarely maintain full standing height throughout the cabin or offer generous lighting and ventilation. Nor are they stocked with all the amenities of home. Still, they provide the boat with important cabin fundamentals, such as marine heads, galleys, berths, and stowage compartments. On large walkarounds, the cabins can be quite substantial and include shore-power electrical hookups, standing showers, microwave ovens, refrigerators, alcohol/butane/electric stoves, tables with bench seats, and many other features typically found on cruising boats.

Unlike low-to-the-water center consoles, walkarounds are medium-height boats, even without towers, antennae, and outriggers. Exterior cabin structures and windscreens raise clearance heights to levels where going under bridges becomes an important concern. On large walkarounds, the measurement for bridge-clearance height can run to more than nine feet.

Like the center console, the exterior cabin structure can be used to integrate design features, such as a bench seat on the foredeck; or, it can be used as an anchor point for mounting antennae, outriggers, Bimini tops, and aluminum towers. Even more so than on center consoles, welded-aluminum towers are frequently found on walkarounds. The most common are T-tops and hard tops. They are

Twin pedestal seats amidships are standard on walkarounds. The helm position is usually to starboard. To port of the dash is a companionway leading into the cuddy.

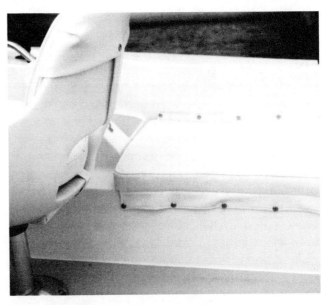

To create additional seating for multiuse walkarounds, some boats fit raised storage compartments with snap-on cushions.

frequently equipped with outriggers and zippered curtains to keep out rain and spray. On bigger boats, towers with spotting platforms and a second set of helm controls are common. Tuna and marlin towers are found on the largest boats in this class. Overall, walkarounds are somewhat longer and beamier than center consoles and more capable of handling a tower without making the boat subject to rock and roll.

Another essential feature of the walkaround is the aft cockpit, which to many fishermen is of much greater importance than the cuddy. As already noted, few fishermen actually use the cuddy for true overnighting, but all fishermen use the cockpit for fighting fish. Here, as on center consoles, wide-open, unobstructed space is highly desired, and walkarounds maximize it by moving the cabin as far forward as possible.

In addition to possessing open space to fight and

land fish, a good cockpit will have integrated fish-fighting features, such as a live-bait well, a fish well, vertical and horizontal rod holders, a tackle-rigging station, and others. It will also be self-bailing, and all wells and below-deck compartments will drain overboard as opposed to running into the bilge. For family fishermen who desire multi-use capability, many builders install aft bench seats, which are sometimes removable, and flip-up transom jump seats. Snap-on pads are also frequently used for the tops of raised storage compartments.

A well-designed cockpit will smoothly flow forward to the midship helm area, which may be located either on the same level as the cockpit deck or raised up a step. The driver's position, complete with dash panel, electronic instruments, and operational controls, is set to starboard and balanced to port by a matching passenger position. Both sides typically feature adjustable swivel seats. A tall windscreen forward of the dash protects both positions, and an entryway, or **companionway,** to the cabin is located between them, usually offset to port.

As previously mentioned, walkarounds are typically outboard powered, although inboard and sterndrive engines are sometimes used, and their hulls generally feature deep or modified Vs. Many of these boats have integrated outboard brackets and most come with full transoms, which prevent swells from flooding the cockpit during a following sea. To work well on transoms without deep cutouts, builders generally require a minimum outboard shaft length of twenty-five inches. Although draft is relatively shallow on typical walkarounds, few fishermen take them into the tidal flats. For the most part, walkarounds are built to stalk deep in-shore, nearshore, and offshore waters.

SMALL WALKAROUNDS

The size range for small walkarounds runs from just under twenty feet to roughly twenty-four feet in length. Beams run from eight feet to nine feet, with a few inches of play either way. Bridge clearance on boats without towers and outriggers ranges from five feet six inches to six feet six inches. Drafts can be anywhere from one foot to three feet, and weights can run from two thousand pounds to four thousand pounds.

Since small walkarounds are capable of running far offshore in good conditions, fuel capacities start at about seventy-five gallons and run to as much as one hundred fifty gallons to provide plenty of range. Bottom configurations are modified-Vs and deep-Vs. Single and twin outboards are the power of choice, and they range in size from 175 horsepower to 400 horsepower. Sterndrive and inboard propulsion systems are sometimes found in this class, but they are rare. Outboards and sterndrives always have hydraulic-assist steering and spin stainless-steel props. Cruising speeds are in the neighborhood of 30 mph, with top speeds in the 40-mph to 50-mph range. Beginning at a low of about twenty thousand dollars, prices can go as high as fifty thousand for a fully outfitted rig.

As offshore boats, walkarounds generally possess either a full transom or one with a tall cutout and a fold-up splashboard. This design helps prevent the possibility of flooding from a following sea. To accommodate tall transoms, outboards are required to have twenty-five-inch or thirty-inch shafts, as opposed to the twenty-inch shafts frequently found on small, inshore skiffs. Outboard transom brackets are also frequently used on boats in this class, which helps free up cockpit space and improve performance. Other frequent transom features are trim tabs, eye hooks (lifting points for davits that are found on most boats smaller than thirty feet long), and swim steps with ladders, which are non-fishing features intended for family use.

Inside the cockpit, the transom is commonly uncluttered to provide plenty of snag-free fish-fighting space. A few transoms may have vertical rod holders, bait wells, and tackle-preparation stations. Non-fishing features found on multiuse boats are a navigation-light mount, removable bench seats, flip-up jump seats, raw-water or freshwater wash-down hoses, and drink holders. Batteries are frequently located in storage boxes at the transom.

The open expanse of the main cockpit typically has a nonskid deck. Scuppers are in the aft corners to facilitate overboard draining. Many boats also have small ports in the deck sole to provide access to the bilge area for maintenance and repairs. Some have below-deck fish boxes. Dual bilge pumps with a capacity of more than 2,000 gph are found on bigger boats. The same is true of fish-fighting chairs, which are still relatively rare in this class.

Beneath the gunwales, better boats have horizontal rod racks, toe rails, and bolster pads on the coam-

A canvas Bimini top or sunshade is a simple method for protecting the captain and crew of a walkaround from the sun and rain.

ing. Mounted on top of the gunwales are rocket launchers, outriggers, radio/loran/GPS antennae, and Bimini-top mounts. Also standard are two sets of cleats; aft cleats, located near the transom, and spring-line cleats, located amidships. The amidships cleat is called the spring-line cleat, because the aft-running line that attaches to it during overnight docking or docking in adverse conditions is called the **spring line.** Hawse pipes for the aft cleats are found on better boats. The height of both the gunwales and the transom (about mid-thigh height) is low enough to give fishermen easy access to the water for netting fish or pulling them in with a **gaff,** a pole with a metal hook end. This gives the boats a low aft profile and a gently rising forward one.

Above-deck features in the cockpit area include insulated fish boxes (found in quality boats), insulated coolers, cockpit lights, and a tackle box, although this unit is somewhat rare in boats of this size. Located in the helm area—the forward part of

the cockpit—are the dash and operational controls. Typical dash instruments and gauges are the same as on center consoles and most fishing boats: speedometer, tachometer, compass, warning lights, oil gauge, fuel gauge, engine-water temperature gauge, oil-pressure gauge, and sometimes, on the better boats, a built-in depth meter. Switches typically found on the dash include: the horn, bilge pump, bilge blower, navigation lights, courtesy lights, live-well aerator, live-well pump, and other accessories. Electronic instruments typically mounted above the dash or overhead are bottom sonar (usually called a fish-finder, chart recorder, video sounder, or a graph recorder), loran-C receiver, and GPS receiver. Operational controls include the ignition, throttle, emergency shut-off device, engine-trim control (for outboards and sterndrives), and trim-tab controls. Boats with engine-trim capability and trim tabs may also have indicator gauges on the dash for each system. The better boats will have a flip-up plastic cover over the dash instruments and gauges to protect them from salt spray.

Standard seating in the helm area is typically twin adjustable swivel seats, and many have either built-in or flip-up footrests. Depending on the size of the boat, other features found in the helm include: radio/cassette player, fire extinguisher, drink holders, grab handles, side storage pockets and compartments, lockable glove boxes (for maps, flashlights, binoculars, and so forth), and lockable below-dash boxes (usually reserved for the VHF radio). Some boats offer an electric wiper on the windscreen.

Walkarounds in this size category typically have a small cabin that sleeps two in a single **V berth,** which refers to a berth located below the foredeck in the bow. Larger boats may have two individual berths. In the smallest cabins, there may be little more than a few horizontal rod holders, interior lights, a few small storage compartments, and two

Full plastic and canvas enclosures or curtains protect a walkaround from the elements. Forward and side curtains alone are often used offshore to keep out spray.

Bow pulpit hardware on larger walkarounds includes bow rails, cleats, anchor roller, and windlass.

small window hatches. Lighting and ventilation are typically minimal.

Cabins in larger walkarounds frequently have a marine head fitted with either a portable or a permanent toilet with a holding tank that has pump-out capability. Large, stand-up head compartments also have a mirror, light, and sink. A galley is also typical in boats of this size, and is generally equipped with a refrigerator, alcohol or butane stove, table with bench seats, and a sink with a small water tank (typically holding no more than ten gallons). Carpeting is also frequently found on the bulkheads and overhead.

Walkarounds with welded-aluminum towers usually bolt them to the exterior of the cuddy or to the surrounding perimeter deck or a combination of both. On smaller boats, the typical tower is a T-top or hard top, occasionally with a spotting platform. Front and side zippered curtains are common options. Those with spotting platforms sometimes fit them with a second set of operational controls. Tall tuna and marlin towers are less frequently seen. As

on center consoles, towers are ideal structures for mounting antennae, radar units, outriggers, rocket launchers, and electronic boxes positioned over the dash. For boats without towers, Bimini tops are virtually standard.

As part of the perimeter deck, the foredeck is easily accessible for bow fishing and docking maneuvers. The chief features found here are a bow pulpit, anchor hardware, cleats, anchor locker, bow rails, navigation light, and, sometimes, a bench seat recessed into the ceiling of the cabin.

LARGE WALKAROUNDS

What makes large walkarounds so attractive compared to small walkarounds is that they have more of everything: on-board space, fish-fighting features, comfort features, and overall protection from heavy weather. While not the ultimate offshore warrior, the large walkaround is probably the next-best thing.

Large walkarounds, generally from twenty-four

feet to thirty-nine feet in length, regularly run fifty miles offshore in all but the foulest conditions. A major factor in their all-weather stability is a wide beam—beginning at eight feet six inches and running to more than twelve feet. Weights run from four thousand pounds to well beyond ten thousand pounds. Bridge-clearance height (without towers or outriggers) starts at less than seven feet and rises to more than nine feet.

Another attractive aspect of large walkarounds is that despite their size, they're still capable of small-boat speed. Typically configured with deep-V hulls (with a few mod Vs) and relatively shallow drafts (from eighteen inches to three feet), these boats get on plane and fly if equipped with enough horsepower. Top speeds in the 45-mph range are common. Average cruising speeds are about 35 mph .

To achieve this kind of performance, the boats have to approach the upper limit of their power curve, which typically runs from 200 horsepower (for single-engine installations) to more than 500 horsepower (for twin engines). Although outboards are still the power of choice in this class (with twenty-five-inch or thirty-inch shafts), inboards are also popular. Among inboards, diesels are frequently found in bigger boats. Sterndrives, as usual, are the least popular fishing-boat propulsion system.

Boats of this size can burn fuel as fast as they can pump it, especially on high-speed runs to offshore hot spots. To offer plenty of range, fuel tanks start at less than one hundred gallons and run to more than three hundred gallons. Prices range from somewhat more than thirty thousand dollars to well into six figures for a fully equipped rig.

So, what does "fully equipped" mean in a large walkaround? In general, it means inclusion of all the features mentioned in connection with small walkarounds, plus quite a few others.

Starting at the transom, this means outboard brackets, either bolted on or molded into the hull. Trim tabs are universal. So is a minimum of twin, high-capacity bilge pumps with a total discharge volume of at least 3,000 gph. Transom doors typically ease the burden of hoisting trophy catches into the fish box. Padded bolsters help soften the edges of the coaming. Live wells, tackle-preparation stations, and wash-down hoses are also standard equipment. Fighting chairs are common. Although the aft sheer line is low enough to reach the water with a net or gaff, it typically rises sharply forward, sometimes with a discernible split sheer.

On multiuse boats, a grab handle and possibly an aluminum ladder help transform the outboard bracket into a swim platform. Snap-on cushions for aft bench seats and hatch-lid seats are also frequently found.

The helm area is usually raised a step or two from the level of the aft cockpit to open up space belowdecks. The area above the dash is typically filled with an array of electronic components, which includes autopilots and navigation plotters that are interfaced with GPS and loran-C receivers. Welded-aluminum towers are more the rule than the exception, and simple Bimini tops are rare. Hard tops are common and frequently fitted with spotting platforms. Many have a second set of controls. On the bigger boats, tower **fly bridges** are sometimes found. These are very high dual-helm positions capable of accommodating more than one person and being equipped with full protection (overhead cover and side curtains). Front and side curtains are common on all boats in this class. The same is true of full bow pulpits with electric **windlasses,** which are winch-type devices used to hoist the anchor.

Walkarounds in this class typically have cabins that are fully carpeted and capable of handling true overnight cruising and multiday offshore runs. They feature full standing height and multiple hatches to provide ventilation and natural light. They also generally have two berths—a double V berth and, at a minimum, a single berth. The bigger boats often have secondary sleeping quarters (called mid or **aft cabins,** because of their location beneath the helm). Aft cabins are characterized by low ceilings, small hatches, and double berths.

Large-cabin walkarounds are frequently equipped with an electrical hookup to plug into AC power while at the dock, which is called a **shore-power hookup.** Galleys in boats like these are typically outfitted with tables, electric stoves, microwaves, copious storage compartments, and refrigerators. Marine heads are fully equipped, too, with showers, electric flushing, macerators, towel racks, and outlets for hair dryers and electric razors. Water tanks generally hold from thirty gallons to fifty gallons. The plushest cabins even come with air conditioning powered by an onboard generator.

Even small cuddy boats with little onboard room to spare place more emphasis on the belowdecks cabin. Note the raised foredeck area that eliminates fishing from the bow.

CUDDY CABINS

Cuddy cabins are one of the most popular designs in boating. They are as at home on fresh water as on salt water, and as useful for cruising as for fishing. In fact, one of the reasons walkarounds work as fishing boats is because they are a modification of the successful cuddy-cabin theme.

But there are clear philosophical differences between the two styles of boat. Chief among these is in the area of multiuse capability. Fishermen looking for a pure, dedicated fishing boat should probably focus on walkarounds. Fishermen who want multiuse versatility may be better served by a cuddy cabin. While walkarounds are versatile fishing boats, they rarely make good platforms for recreational boating. Cuddys, on the other hand, can be outfitted equally well for plush comfort or hard-core fishing.

In boats outfitted primarily for fishing, the differences between cuddies and walkarounds are relatively small. The biggest differences are found on the side decks and foredeck. Instead of a recessed, nonskid, 360° walking deck located at approximately the same level as the aft cockpit, cuddy boats simply use the topside of the cabin for the foredeck and unprotected gunwales for the side decks. In some boats, the catwalks are too narrow to safely walk on, and builders install walk-through windscreens for access to the bow.

Another difference between walkarounds and cuddies is found in the cabin itself. Cabins on cuddies tend to be larger and sacrifice some top space for belowdecks and helm comfort. This doesn't mean that cuddy-cabin interiors are spacious, but it means that whenever possible, cuddy boats tend to favor multiuse comfort. This becomes evident in positioning the cuddy farther aft and making the side decks narrow.

Cuddy fishing boats range from as small as nineteen feet to as big as thirty-five feet. Beams start at seven feet six inches and run to well beyond ten feet. Drafts go from eighteen inches to more than three feet. Weights can be as slim as twenty-five hundred pounds and run well beyond ten thousand pounds.

To provide plenty of side-to-side stability in rolling seas, cuddies tend to produce more mod-V hulls than deep-V hulls, although both are common. Fuel-tank capacities run from fifty gallons to three hundred gallons, depending on the size of boat. Typical propulsion systems on cuddies split about evenly between inboards/sterndrives and outboards. Standard engines start as low as 150 horsepower and max out at more than 600 horsepower. Cruising speeds are about 30 mph; top speeds rarely exceed the low 40s, except for tournament kingfish boats that top out in the low 60s. Sticker prices begin at less than twenty-five thousand dollars and run well into the low six figures.

As mentioned, total cabin area on cuddies tends to be relatively more spacious than on walkarounds. Still, interior standing height is usually limited, and sleeping quarters rarely exceed four persons, even on the biggest boats, which frequently put a midship sleeping cabin under the raised helm. Rather than true overnight cruising, most cuddy cabins are simply used for refuge from the weather, afternoon naps, and lockable storage that's protected from the elements.

As noted, cuddies can be outfitted with full fishing rigging, including rocket launchers, tackle-preparation stations, integrated tackle drawers, fish boxes, bait wells, fighting chairs, outriggers, rod racks, transom doors, welded-aluminum towers, flying bridges, and all the rest. They can also feature lean-and-mean cabins or plush ones with shore-power hookups, electronic accessories, carpeting, full galleys, full marine heads, twin double berths, and much more.

Since they are true offshore boats, cuddies are

Fishing is intended to be limited to the cockpit of a cuddy boat, which is usually large enough for the purpose. Access to the foredeck is accomplished by walking narrow, unprotected gunwales.

typically outfitted with a well-equipped helm station that includes trim-tab controls (trim tabs are virtually standard); full engine instrumentation; covered chart tables; lockable storage boxes; and a full complement of electronic instruments—depth/fish sonars, VHF radios, radio/cassette/CD players, radar units, GPS receivers, loran-C receivers, plotters, and sometimes, autopilots. Seating in the helm is similar to a walkaround, with twin adjustable swivel chairs, but there is more space, due to the narrower side decks.

In the big-boat classes, the ability to spend quality time with family and friends becomes an increasingly important consideration. Walkarounds and cuddy cabins are the most popular midsize saltwater fishing boats, because they perform both fishing and cruising functions equally well in a package that's low on maintenance and still comparatively affordable.

CHAPTER 4

BATTLE WAGONS: CONVERTIBLE SPORTFISHERMEN

When most people think of serious offshore fishing boats—wave-busting, fish-battling war wagons—they typically think of a class of boats known as convertibles, the pride of saltwater marinas. These boats are instantly recognizable with their tall flying bridges, huge tuna towers, a skyline of antennae and outriggers, large salons and cabins, and a forest of rocket launchers loaded with gleaming heavy-duty tackle. Not only are these head-turners the best fishing boats money can buy; they have also played a central role in the historical development of recreational saltwater fishing.

While the modern version of offshore sportfishing can be dated to the mid 1970s, when form, function, and technology converged with affordability, the birth of the sport itself dates to the late 1940s. True, offshore anglers fished for sport well before the 1940s. Equally true, there were early pioneers such as Hemingway, Zane Gray, and others (including many influential guides and captains from Florida and California) who helped popularize the sport. And, finally, there's little doubt that many of these giants helped advance sportfishing in such important areas as design, technology, and technique.

But none would deny the pivotal role played by one dedicated fisherman, conservationist, and designer, John Rybovich, father of the most impressive class of sportfishing boats on the water—the convertible sportfisherman. Basically, a **convertible** is a high-performance, extended-cruising, saltwater fishing boat. And although Rybovich became noted for creating the "Mother Superior" of all convertibles at his West Palm Beach, Florida, boatyard, he didn't actually coin the term itself.

The king of the offshore recreational fleet and pride of saltwater marinas is the largest class of saltwater fishing boats—the convertible.

Convertible was coined in the late 1950s by Willis Slane and a fledgling North Carolina company by the name of Hatteras Yachts, which made a name for itself as pioneer in building large fiberglass fishing boats and yachts. Early in its career, Hatteras thought it needed to jump-start its reputation by appealing to as many potential buyers as possible. With this in mind, Slane came up with the word *convertible* to describe a new kind of boat that was suitable for both serious cruising and serious fishing. Despite the vagueness of the term, it stuck, and many other builders quickly followed suit (Bertram, Trojan, Viking, and Luhrs to name a few).

John Rybovich, on the other hand, never called his boats convertibles. He simply called them sportfishermen. Until his death in 1993, Rybovich considered the term to be a misnomer. Even though his boats were often referred to as convertibles, the famed yard of Rybovich and Sons (which is still in operation after several changes in ownership) never actually built dual-purpose boats. The classic wooden boats built by Rybovich were fishing boats first and foremost, and ultimately defined the genre. Virtually everything that composes a modern convertible, except for fiberglass construction, derives from the boats that John Rybovich (along with his brothers Tommy and Emil) designed and built for adventurous clients in the late 1940s and early 1950s.

Rybovich began his assault on the status quo of saltwater fishing boats in 1947 with the design of *Miss Chevy II*. While Rybovich insists that this boat was little different from other open-cockpit, trunk-cabin gamefish boats of the day, it already had trademark convertible characteristics, such as extensive use of rot-resistant teak, cockpit toe rails, rounded corners to soften edges, hawse pipes, a flying bridge, fighting chair, and aluminum outriggers. All of these now-familiar components (which were innovations at the time) can be traced to the Rybovich yards, and most appeared for the first time on *Miss Chevy II*.

Despite the importance of *Miss Chevy II* in boating history, the first true Rybo convertible, according to the designer himself, was *Miss Chevy IV*, built in 1952. In this boat, the familiar profile of the modern convertible, with its large flybridge deck, tuna tower, and extended split sheer, was instantly recognizable. This boat also served to introduce the open-

Note the flat sheer line aft that leads to the low-freeboard cockpit, and the rising sheer line that leads forward to the high-freeboard foredeck. This is a classic split sheer, which is something of a tradition on convertibles.

ing transom door, a useful feature for pulling in fish. The transom door forever replaced side-mounted or transom-mounted pole-and-roller systems. *Miss Chevy IV,* which also integrated other innovative features found on earlier Rybos, is known as the prototype for the modern-day sportfishing boat.

As noted, Rybovich frequently said that he was not interested in creating dual-purpose boats, yet as the 1950s wore on and transitioned into the 1960s, his boats became equipped with increasingly large deckhouses and enclosed salons. (A **salon** is a carpeted and air-conditioned living area with a lounge and dinette.) According to Rybovich, his purpose in designing these boats was not to make them yacht-like, but to give their owners an edge in winning fishing tournaments by improving their capacity for long-range cruising.

Through the late 1940s and most of the 1950s, Rybovich built what he considered day boats. Nearport fishing was so good that long-range trips were virtually unnecessary. This point is illustrated in the two *Miss Chevy* boats, which were less than thirty-seven feet long, ran no faster than twenty knots, and were built with cabins that could fit little more than a couple of berths, a head, galley, and stowage compartments. The dinette and lounge were actually located outside the cabin in an open salon.

By the late 1950s, however, it became necessary to build long-range boats for two reasons: Fish were starting to become more scarce, so anglers were increasingly forced to make one-way runs of twenty to thirty miles to be competitive; and Cuba and the Bahamas were becoming more popular, which meant that boats had to be capable of making ninety-mile open-water runs. To enable anglers to handle these runs in rugged weather, Rybovich began building bigger, beamier boats with more powerful engines. Then he enclosed the salons and enlarged the deckhouses. This completed the evolution of the original gamefish day boat into the modern bluewater convertible.

In the end, however, neither Rybovich's designation (cruising sportfisherman) nor the commonly accepted term (convertible) seems to hit the nail on the head. Both seem too vague to describe a definitive class of boat. Until someone comes up with a better name, perhaps the best approach is to combine the best of each and call them convertible sportfishermen.

THE FLYBRIDGE

At first glance, nothing so defines a convertible sportfishing boat as a **flybridge,** a shortened form of the old shipping term *flying bridge,* which refers to the highest navigational bridge or helm on a ship. On a modern sportfishing convertible, a flybridge is a raised deck that's located above the cabin and functions either as the main navigational helm or as the secondary helm.

For recreational boats, the flybridge originally came out of the world of cruising yachts. It was added to the vocabulary of fishing boats in the 1950s when gamefish became harder to find, especially tuna and marlin. For fishermen to remain competitive, a tall vantage point for long-distance spotting became crucial. At first, builders simply modified existing boats by reinforcing cabin roofs and converting them into raised helms or bridges (as was done on *Pilar*), but before long, build-

The well-equipped control console on a typical raised bridge.

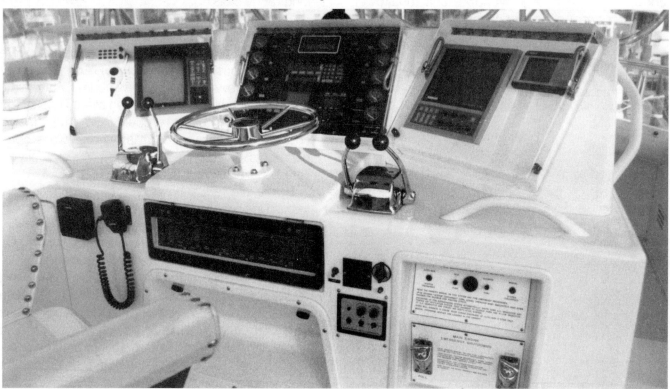

ers began designing boats with integrated fly-bridges.

Unlike smaller classes of boats, helm stations on convertibles are not offset starboard, but are typically located amidships for optimum 360° visibility around the boat. Like all hard-core fishing boats, these helms have few accommodations other than a centerline-mounted captain's chair and, possibly, a companion chair and an aft railing, where rocket launchers are frequently mounted. On bigger convertibles, there may be a bench or L-shaped lounge seat, a cooler, and storage compartments. True windshields are rarely found on flybridge decks, but some feature low, venturitype windscreens.

To reach the bridge, the captain and crew climb an external aluminum ladder from the aft cockpit. On very large convertibles, there may be an internal stairway. Once on the bridge, which is located a full story above the cockpit and main deck, the captain has an excellent long-range view of the water and also down into the cockpit. Once a fish is hooked,

With controls located on the raised bridge, there is nothing to gain by installing a forward deckhouse windshield. In fact, it could be a liability in high seas when waves break over the bow.

the captain's main focus shifts aft. With one eye on the fish and one eye on the fishermen, the captain typically works the throttles by standing with his back to the control panel. Consequently, a well-designed bridge will be positioned so that sightlines are as clean aft as they are forward.

With boat operation and navigation the primary

A tall tuna tower rises more than two stories above the raised bridge. A marlin tower is generally somewhat shorter.

duties of the helm, you can bet that most convertibles are outfitted with virtually all the electronic instruments and gauges known to man. To accommodate this array, helms are fitted with substantial consoles (many with adjacent chart tables), dash panels, and overhead electronic boxes (mounted to hard tops).

Instruments and gauges typically found on convertibles include such fishing-boat standards as compasses (magnetic or electric), VHF radios, depth/fish-finding sonar, GPS receivers, loran receivers, and radar. Other big-boat items (discussed in detail in Chapter 6) include single-side band (SSB) radios (for long-range communication); autopilots; CB radios; fuel-monitoring systems; complete boat-warning systems; hailers (for ship-to-ship or ship-to-dock communication); EPIRBS (emergency satellite broadcasters); chart plotters (electronic units that perform route planning and other navigational operations by using input from other instruments, such as radar, GPS, loran, and so forth); and sea-temperature indicators and weather facsimile recorders (which print out charts and satellite images transmitted from shoreside stations).

A few flybridge convertibles have second helm stations located immediately below the bridge. This arrangement creates a sheltered navigation area for captains in foul weather, and requires the installation of a windshield in the forward wall of the deckhouse. To some serious fishermen, a deckhouse windshield can be a boat's weak link, especially in heavy weather when green water sometimes crashes over the bow. To cope with this possibility, many convertibles forgo deckhouse windshields in favor of a solid forward wall of reinforced fiberglass.

On boats like these, a second helm station is typically located high above the bridge in a tuna tower. Unlike such weight-sensitive boats as walkarounds and center consoles, convertibles are able to support considerable weight aloft, including two or more hard decks and a hard top above the tallest set of controls. Some boats take this concept to the extreme by raising a crow's nest as much as forty feet above the water. Towers of this weight can be dangerous to use in rough weather, and are recommended only for fish-fighting scenarios. Zippered side and forward curtains are standard for most flybridge and tower perches. Radar arches and outriggers are also common.

MULTIPLE DECKS

With the addition of flybridges and enlarged deckhouses, designers of convertibles were forced to alter the basic layout of the typical offshore fishing boat. This development had an impact on many elements of a convertible's design, but none more so than the size and shape of the cockpit and deckhouse cabin.

To make this new class of boat a truly dedicated sportfisherman, designers had to be careful not to favor comfort and luxury over fishing features, which is typically done with flybridge cruisers and motoryachts. Designers accomplished this feat by expanding the size of the aft cockpit in relation to cockpits in cruising boats, and by reducing the size and complexity of the main deck. The result is a boat with three important characteristics: an uncompromising fish-fighting cockpit; an enclosed deckhouse that provides excellent shelter and overnighting capability for at least a crew of four; and weight sensitivity (exemplified in the reduced size of the deckhouse in relation to cruising yachts) to improve overall performance.

Cockpit design follows the basic principles in convertibles as previously discussed in walkarounds and cabin boats, except that they are carried out in Olympian style. Starting in the neighborhood of one hundred square feet in smaller boats, convertible cockpits run all the way up to two hundred feet in megaconvertibles. Equipment ranges from ice chests integrated into deck fish boxes to twin fighting chairs to transom doors and all the other expected amenities. But to be truly functional, a good cockpit must feature unobstructed space and snag-free surfaces—and it must be low enough to enable fishermen to reach the water with a net or gaff.

Because of low-to-the-water gunwales, convertible cockpit decks are usually several steps lower than the main deck. By raising the main deck, designers create a lower deck for the engine room (amidships) and staterooms or sleeping quarters (forward). The engine room is typically reachable from the aft cockpit. The staterooms are accessed through the deckhouse.

As noted, the main purpose of the deckhouse is to provide comfortable shelter for long-range runs. While convertibles aren't necessarily equipped with all the comforts of home, especially in comparison with cruising yachts, they aren't exactly shabby. The deckhouse on a typical convertible comes with a carpeted salon complete with a living-room-style lounge and dinette, plus a relatively well-equipped galley. Galleys usually feature such items as electric ovens, electric ranges, microwave ovens, storage cabinets, sinks, refrigerators, and ice makers. Salons usually have L-shaped sofas, chairs, TVs, radio/cassette/CD players, air conditioning, heat, screen doors, window blinds, tinted safety-glass windows, indirect lighting, central vacuuming, and many other features.

The lower deck, as already mentioned, is composed of two main areas: the engine room and the sleeping quarters. Although the engine room rarely features full standing height, most compartments are large enough to walk into (if hunched over) to access the powerplants, plumbing systems, and electrical systems for maintenance and repair.

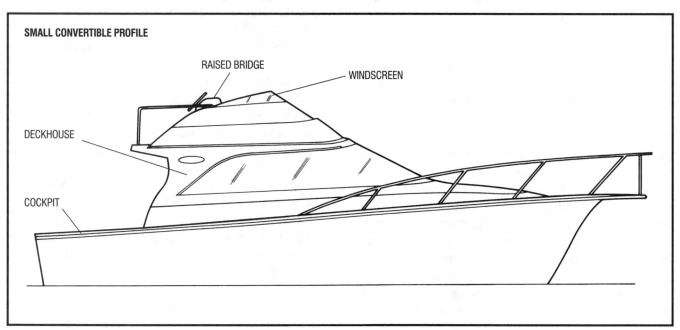

SMALL CONVERTIBLE PROFILE

RAISED BRIDGE

WINDSCREEN

DECKHOUSE

COCKPIT

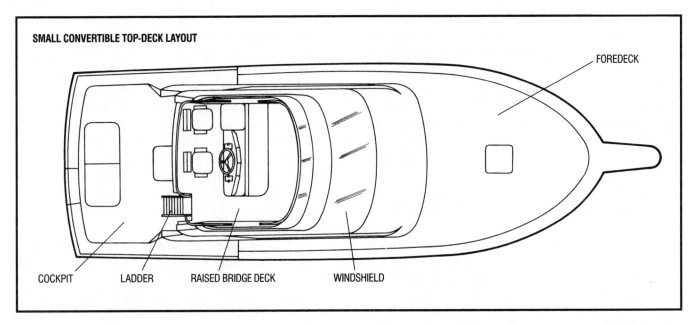

SMALL CONVERTIBLE TOP-DECK LAYOUT

FOREDECK

COCKPIT   LADDER   RAISED BRIDGE DECK   WINDSHIELD

SMALL CONVERTIBLES

Because of their large architectural elements—cockpits, flybridges, deckhouses, and staterooms—convertibles by definition are sizable boats. However, some builders attempt to squeeze everything into a pint-size package. Rather than calling these boats convertibles, a more accurate name would be *flybridge sportfishermen* or *pocket convertibles*. Many of these boats have open salons instead of fully enclosed deckhouses; single-person spotting platforms instead of multipassenger crow's nest helms; and small flybridge decks.

Genuine small convertibles, which are capable of running one hundred or more miles offshore and tackling heavy weather in the open ocean, begin in the neighborhood of thirty feet and run to thirty-nine feet long. Beams start at more than ten feet and run to more than fourteen feet. Bridge clearance (without towers and outriggers) ranges from about eleven feet to thirteen feet. Drafts average about three feet, with six inches of variation either way.

Weight runs from ten thousand pounds to more than twenty thousand pounds. And to give these convertibles the range they need, fuel tanks start at one hundred sixty gallons and run to more than four hundred gallons.

Since convertibles are built for long-range runs, they usually come with large, twin-engine propulsion systems. Power of choice is a twin inboard installation. Diesel engines are popular because of their renowned reputation for long-term reliability and fuel efficiency. The typical power package runs from about 500 horsepower to nearly 900 horsepower, with top speeds of just under 40 mph. Props on boats like these are typically made of **Nibral,** an alloy composed of nickel, bronze, and aluminum. Modified-V and deep-V hulls help these boats knife through the rollers, although a few convertibles opt for shallow-V hulls to improve side-to-side stability and reduce the tendency to rock and roll while drifting or slow trolling.

The price range for convertibles is difficult to pin down, because this class is so heavily influenced by semicustom boats, and buyers rarely pick up a ready-made convertible from a boatyard lot. While the fundamental architecture can't be changed, virtually everything else can—including the engines, number of staterooms, deckhouse layout, interior appointments, flybridge layout, electronics package, and many other options. Still, most builders start with a base price and then offer their customers a list of options. Using base-boat figures, small convertibles start at about one hundred twenty thousand dollars and go to well beyond the two-hundred-thousand mark. However, to boaters who really want to exhaust their bank accounts, these parameters can seem like pocket change.

As noted, the smallest boats in this class run a fine line between being flybridge sportfishermen and true convertibles, but even the smallest come with aft cockpits in the neighborhood of one hundred square feet. Standard features typically include rod holders, live wells, side-locker storage compartments, tackle lockers, transom doors, seawater and freshwater wash-down hookups, padded bolsters for the coaming, tackle-rigging stations, and dock-side-water hookups. In addition, many cockpits come with insulated fish boxes (sometimes refrigerated or made into a freezer), ice makers, boarding steps, fighting chairs, teak decks and trim, and many other offerings.

The engine room, located either beneath the aft portion of the cockpit (in small convertibles) or beneath the salon on the main deck, is the heart of the boat. It is dominated by twin diesel powerplants, and also contains core units for the plumbing and electrical systems. These include a gas or diesel electrical generator (or **genset**), a converter, multiple batteries, cold-water pump, air-conditioning unit, heating unit, and a hot-water heater. Also standard is a fire warning and extinguisher system.

As already noted, standard equipment on a typical convertible flybridge contains all the navigation, operation, and fishing features known to man. Without repeating the long list of familiar instruments and gauges, suffice it to say that everything from radar to SSB radios to plotters to hydraulic steering

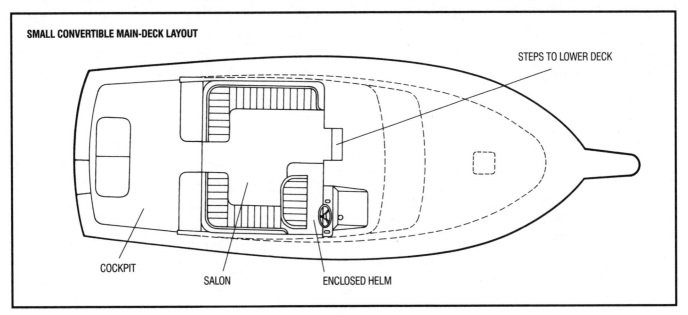

SMALL CONVERTIBLE MAIN-DECK LAYOUT

STEPS TO LOWER DECK

COCKPIT

SALON

ENCLOSED HELM

to complete electrical warning systems are found at the helm of a typical convertible. To accommodate these instruments, helm consoles are fairly large and frequently incorporate flat navigation tables. Overhead electronics boxes are also common. Radar arches, hard tops, and towers with a second set of operational controls are frequently found on boats of this size. In the crow's-nest station, only vital controls are needed, such as throttles, trim-tab controls, ignition, depth-sounder, tachometer, engine water temperature gauge, fuel gauge, engine-warning lights, VHF radio, intercom, and a few

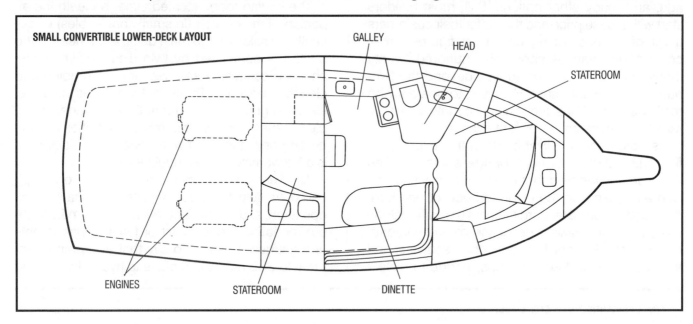

SMALL CONVERTIBLE LOWER-DECK LAYOUT

GALLEY
HEAD
STATEROOM
ENGINES
STATEROOM
DINETTE

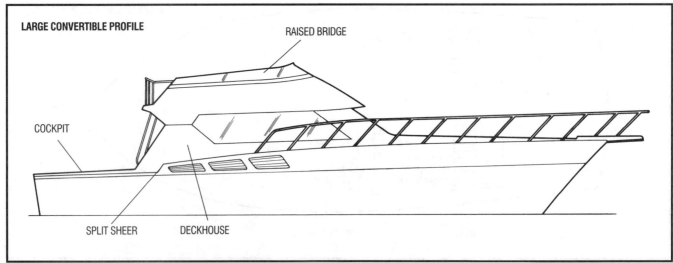

LARGE CONVERTIBLE PROFILE

RAISED BRIDGE
COCKPIT
SPLIT SHEER
DECKHOUSE

others. Other features sometimes found in this perch are leaning posts, belly rails, sunshades, and hard tops.

On small convertibles, a typical main-deck layout includes an aft salon, which can be converted to a dinette and sleeping berths, plus the main helm station. All areas are fully carpeted. The galley on boats like this is usually found on the lower deck. In larger boats, the main helm area may be located in an isolated pilot house. On boats without a forward windshield, the galley replaces the interior helm. The head and two staterooms, one of which is outfitted with over/under bunks and one with double berths, are typically located beneath the foredeck on a carpeted lower-deck level. The main sleeping quarters, or master stateroom, usually comes with a mirror, private head, closets, and drawers. Dedicated sleeping quarters for four is typical in boats of this class. Additional berths can be made out of the lounge sofa.

Other features common to convertibles of this size include freshwater tanks (fifty gallons to eighty gallons), bow rails, hatches on the foredeck,

anchor pulpits with windlasses, canvas coverings for the cockpit and raised bridge, shore-power hookups, telephone jacks, and television.

While bigger is often better in offshore boating, there is one area where smaller convertibles are frequently a step ahead of their larger cousins—the foredeck. On many convertibles (both large and small), the foredeck is just a big skating-rink surface that's only used as a means to get to the anchor and bowlines. However, some convertibles, typically small ones, put a nonskid pattern on the foredeck and install tall bow rails. This effectively turns a large wasted area into a bow platform for bottom fishing. Boats like these also have wide, walkable side decks. Some, especially on the West Coast, even have bow-mounted live wells.

LARGE CONVERTIBLES

While we can pin down forty feet as the beginning length for large convertibles, the upper parameter runs off the chart. One-of-a-kind custom boats oc-

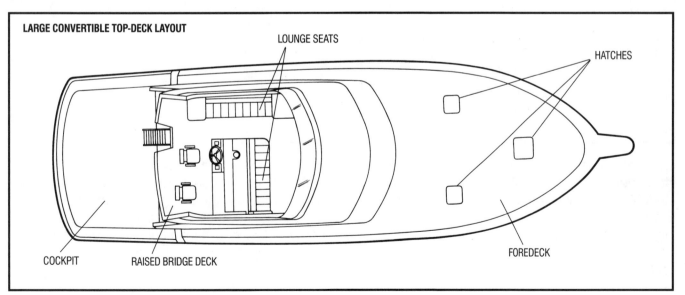

LARGE CONVERTIBLE TOP-DECK LAYOUT

LOUNGE SEATS

HATCHES

COCKPIT　　RAISED BRIDGE DECK

FOREDECK

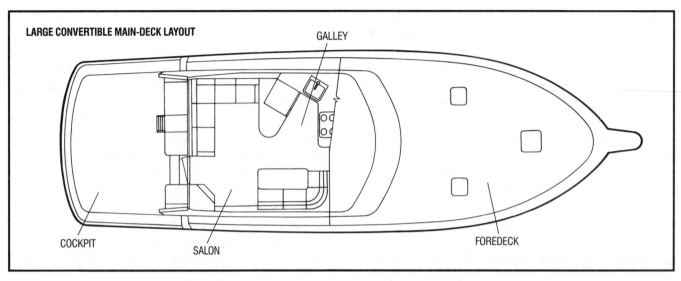

LARGE CONVERTIBLE MAIN-DECK LAYOUT

GALLEY

COCKPIT

SALON

FOREDECK

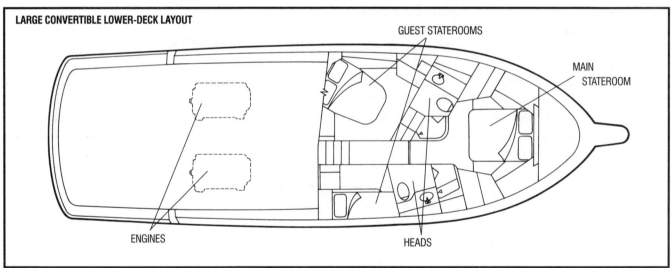

LARGE CONVERTIBLE LOWER-DECK LAYOUT

GUEST STATEROOMS

MAIN STATEROOM

ENGINES

HEADS

casionally break the hundred-foot mark, and why stop there? Boats of this length are guilty of stretching the definition and intent of the convertible class to the breaking point. Typical fish-fighting maneuvers like backing down, fast pivoting, trolling, and kite fishing become difficult in mega-yachts. Owners of these boats would probably be better served by purchasing a motor yacht with an extended cockpit instead of a convertible.

Beams on big convertibles are substantial—running from about thirteen feet to twenty feet. Bridge clearance isn't much different from that on small convertibles, except for a couple of extra feet found on the largest boats (in the neighborhood of fifteen feet).

Most boats in this class come equipped with hard

tops, radar arches or towers, plus a pair of giant out-riggers. Drafts run from four feet to six feet. Weights for boats of this size are typically listed in terms of **displacement,** a measurement that indicates the weight of water that a floating boat displaces. Beginning at twenty-five thousand pounds, the displacement for boats like these runs well into six figures. Displacements for megaconvertibles runs considerably higher.

Large convertibles require big diesel engines that produce a power range from 700 to 3,000 horsepower. Feeding these monsters a steady flow of fuel are tanks that run from three hundred gallons to more than four thousand gallons. Top speed for boats of this size is about 35 mph; cruising speed is typically 20 mph or less. Hull configurations on such large, heavy boats exhibit both planing and semidisplacement characteristics. Most fall into the modified-V category, with a fair number of deep-Vs and shallow-V hulls.

Prices for this imperial class of convertibles are even more difficult to estimate than for their smaller cousins, because virtually everything is customer ordered. But for the sake of establishing rough parameters, consider a quarter-million dollars to be the starting point for the smallest, most stripped-down boat in this class and move well above the million-dollar mark for the upper end of the bracket. Megaconvertibles are in a class by themselves, and are true multimillion-dollar yachts.

There's little to add to the list of features and accommodations for these boats that hasn't already been mentioned, except for such yachtlike features as: isolated crew quarters; standing headroom on all decks; fully enclosed flybridge decks; internal stairways to the flybridge; sunshade extensions over the aft portion of the cockpit; companion seats and lounges on the raised bridge deck; clothes washers and dryers; freshwater tanks that hold between one hundred and eight hundred gallons; split-level galleys; heads with tubs; queen-size berths; whirlpools and saunas; and too many other extras to mention. Boats of this size sleep six to eight comfortably; megaconvertibles can sleep many more.

If price weren't a factor, few offshore fishermen would leave the jetty in anything but a battle-ready convertible. While not possessing the go-anywhere versatility of smaller rigs, no fishing boat is better equipped to make hundred-mile offshore runs and bring crews safely back to port in the worst of conditions. Fully outfitted convertibles, with their wide beams, tall profiles, and gracefully curving sheer lines, are truly the stuff of which fishermen's dreams are made.

CHAPTER 5

FLATS BOATS, EXPRESS BOATS, AND OTHER HYBRIDS

What makes a saltwater fishing boat a modern classic? For starters, a marriage of form and function that produces a boat of superior seaworthiness, performance, and fishability. Second, an appeal so strong that it wins over converts among fishermen and builders. And, finally, a track record of national success that's maintained for a number of years.

By this standard, center consoles, walkarounds, and convertibles are certainly classics. But there are many other familiar fishing boats that prowl the waterways and catch fish each year. Many are based on designs that have been around for decades. Quite a few are beautifully crafted and marvelously functional. Why aren't these boats modern classics?

Primarily because many of these boats are regional favorites, such as flats boats, rolled-edge skiffs, and pilothouse boats. Many others are hy-

Stalking wary prey in the shallow water of a tidal flat requires a lightweight, flat-bottom boat that can be pushed by a fisherman standing on a poling platform.

brids, which mean they combine fishing-boat features with atypical elements usually seen in cruisers, runabouts, or other classic designs. Express boats, dual consoles, and flybridges come to mind in this category. Still others are custom or semicustom boats that are unique unto themselves, and uniqueness does not a classic make.

However, it's important to note that all fishing boats, even widely acknowledged classics, were probably considered hybrids when first introduced. Center consoles, for example, share many characteristics with skiffs. Walkarounds borrow many traits from cuddy-cabin boats and center consoles. And convertibles adapt a number of elements from cruisers.

But all classic designs have two things in common: large numbers of units sold, and many years of nationwide success. Look at it this way: If becoming a classic saltwater fishing boat were decided by election and fishermen voted with their checkbooks, then the boats covered in the previous chapters would be clear winners.

This doesn't mean that other boats aren't good saltwater fishing rigs. It just means that what makes them work so well in some situations, such as sneaking into shallow tidal flats, may not necessarily be beneficial in others, such as running miles offshore. Or it might mean that what makes a multiuse rig work so well in family situations may not be ideal for hard-core fishermen. Boats that compromise their fishability or limit their go-anywhere versatility have difficulty achieving modern classic status.

Still, the following boats are quite popular in their own right, with both fishermen and builders (mostly regional, but national in some cases). No doubt, several boats are modern classics in the making.

FLATS BOATS

The boat with the most legitimate claim to classic status is the **flats boat,** a regional hybrid originally from Florida that dates to the 1950s. Like center-console boats, flats boats evolved from small, wooden, outboard-powered skiffs. They first became popular in the Florida Keys. By the early 1960s, Miami-based fisherman Bob Hewes began building a line of fiberglass flats boats that ultimately defined the class. Soon, other Florida builders joined the competition, and eventually, the design

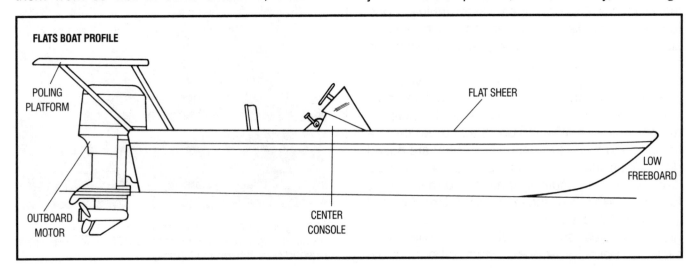

FLATS BOAT PROFILE

POLING PLATFORM

FLAT SHEER

LOW FREEBOARD

OUTBOARD MOTOR

CENTER CONSOLE

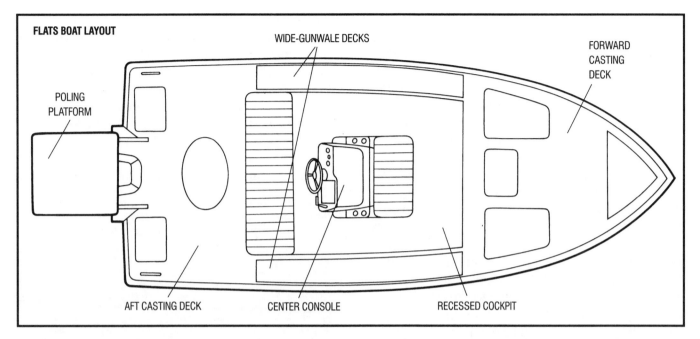

FLATS BOAT LAYOUT

WIDE-GUNWALE DECKS

FORWARD CASTING DECK

POLING PLATFORM

AFT CASTING DECK

CENTER CONSOLE

RECESSED COCKPIT

spread to Louisiana, Texas, and the Carolinas. Today, several national manufacturers have added flats boats to their lines. While the design is more than three decades old, flats boats are currently considered among the hottest saltwater fishing boats in the country and their fame is rapidly spreading to all three coasts.

So what is a flats boat? Flats boats are the smallest of all dedicated saltwater fishing rigs. Lengths run from sixteen feet to twenty feet. Beams are between seven and eight feet. Weights range from nine hundred to fourteen hundred pounds. And drafts are minimal—a foot or less—to help fishermen run in skinny tidal waters.

Diminutive size and heft makes flats boats shallow-water specialists, a niche now benefiting from the current boom in light-tackle angling. To reach shallow, fish-rich marshes, sandbars, and mangrove islands, a flats boat needs to be able to run in less than two feet of water. Also, it must be light enough to maneuver with the engine shut down by means

of pushing on a fiberglass pole. This kind of silent stalking is necessary, because typical shallow-water fish, such as snook, redfish, bonefish, and permit, are wary prey that flee at the first sign (sight or sound) of a fisherman.

As a result of these unique circumstances, flats fishing is line-of-sight fishing, and a **poling platform** is an essential component. A poling platform is a small stand mounted on four aluminum legs, raised approximately three feet above the outboard motor. It measures about six square feet, give or take a foot. A guide or partner stands on the platform and gently uses the pole to maneuver the boat around the flat. At the same time, the guide uses the platform's height advantage to scout the waters for signs of fish.

Since flats boats aren't intended to run in churning offshore waters, they are typically characterized by low freeboard and flat profiles. Short transoms enable them to use outboards with standard twenty-inch shafts. Single outboards are the power of choice, and they typically range from 115 horse-power to 200 horsepower, which makes these rigs 50-mph boats. Fuel capacity is typically limited to the neighborhood of forty-five gallons. Bottom con-figurations are universally shallow-Vs. Some incor-porate flat planing pads at the keel. While base boat prices can be as low as ten thousand dollars, fully equipped rigs with engines and full electronic pack-ages typically cost about twice that amount.

Other essential flats-boat features are a recessed cockpit amidships, a control console, wide gunwale decks, and fore and aft casting decks. Unlike cen-ter-console boats, which have one raised casting deck forward, flats boats have two gunwale-to-gun-wale decks. These casting platforms are important because they elevate fishermen above the cockpit for improved visibility and room to cast in all direc-tions. When used by a crew of two, one angler as-sumes the guide position on the poling platform and the second angler fishes from the forward deck. Both decks are used when the boats are taken out by crews of three or more.

In addition to a molded nonskid surface, these platforms typically have built-in storage lockers, coolers, and live wells in recessed compartments. To maintain a snag-free design, flats boats typically offer minimal deck hardware. Tying up is done by using the bow eye, transom lifting hooks, or poling-platform legs.

Gunwale decks on these boats are designed to be wide enough to stand on while landing a fish. Typical widths are a foot or more. Combined with the casting decks, the side decks give flats boats full-perimeter fishability. Typically, the starboard gun-wale deck is fitted with unobtrusive tie-downs or hooks for securing the pole while under way.

Few features are found in the recessed cockpit area, which in recent years is shrinking in size rela-tive to the raised decks. In keeping with the tradition established by original Florida Keys boats, modern

flats boats are driven either while sitting on the aft deck or standing. For comfort, many boats now have snap-on bench pads or flip-up bench seats. The cockpit sole, aside from the console, is typically free of obstruction, and provides a perfect place for tackle boxes and coolers (sometimes held in place by shock cords). Horizontal rod holders are built into the side bulkheads beneath the gunwales.

While the original Florida flats boats placed the control console to starboard, most modern rigs

Despite its modest size, a well-designed center console on a flats boat can be well equipped with controls, instruments, gauges, and storage compartments.

have a center-console design. Although small, these units are able to accommodate throttles, ignitions, dash panels with operational instruments and gauges, switches for accessories, and tabletop areas for locating a compass and electronic instruments. Antennae and vertical rod holders are typically fitted to the sides of the console. Most feature interior storage compartments.

Bimini tops or canvas sunshades are infrequently used on flats boats. Towers are nonexistent. This doesn't mean, however, that flats boats are bare-bones hulls. On the contrary, well-equipped rigs are loaded with a number of features, including trim tabs, electric trolling motors, heavy-duty bilge pumps, cast-net lockers, VHF radios, loran and GPS receivers, depth and fish sonar, fuel-management gauges, multiple live wells, jack plates for running in skinny water, and many other items.

While Pacific Coast fishermen, with their deep, unprotected shorelines, aren't likely to embrace flats boats with the same enthusiasm that East and Gulf Coast fishermen have in recent years, the future of

Although express boats lack the protection of deck-houses and the raised sightlines of flying bridges, this versatile class can adjust by adding marlin towers and curtain enclosures.

this formerly regional design is bright. Many inland fishermen have become converts because they realize that flats boats are ideal for performing both freshwater and saltwater duty. The same characteristics that work so well on tidal flats also work for maneuvering in freshwater weed beds. And since flats boats are trailerable, freshwater fishermen within a hundred miles of the Gulf Coast and East Coast can double their fishing horizons. Finally, since flats boats are built for harsh saltwater, they are basically overbuilt by freshwater standards and represent a top value, even for fishermen as far away from saltwater as those located on the Great Lakes.

EXPRESS FISHERMEN

Another hybrid boat with an increasingly legitimate claim to classic status is the **express boat,** also known as an open boat, an open express, or an express fisherman. The basic express design, which works well in both medium and large hulls, is composed of an open cockpit and helm located on a single level, plus a full cabin located a few steps below the main deck. While an argument can be made that boats of this type have been around since wooden, trunk-cabin boats were first adapted to offshore fishing, it's only in the last twenty years that these versatile sportfishing rigs have emerged as popular favorites.

The hallmark of an express boat is a wide-open cockpit that leads directly to a helm station located on the same level or raised up a step or two. This layout places the entire crew on a single deck rather than splitting up the fishermen and captain on two different levels (as on flybridge boats and convertibles). The arrangement improves communication when fish are on the line and allows freedom of movement between the helm and cockpit when quick action is needed. Both of these characteristics

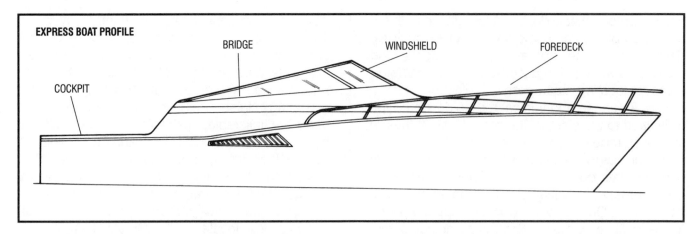

EXPRESS BOAT PROFILE

COCKPIT — BRIDGE — WINDSHIELD — FOREDECK

make expresses ideal for short-handed fishing.

Like smaller, cuddy-cabin boats, expresses are without wide, protected perimeter side decks, the trademark of the walkaround. Instead, the crew walks on the gunwales to reach the bow pulpit for anchoring and docking duties. Unlike cuddy-cabin boats, expresses are typically powered by inboard engines (rarely by outboards and sterndrives). Cuddy cabins are split fairly evenly among outboards, sterndrives, and inboards. As far as size

goes, expresses are roughly equivalent to convertibles in length and beam, perhaps a bit smaller. Cuddy cabins are smaller yet.

In general, express boats range from about twenty-five feet in length to nearly sixty feet. Beams run from eight feet six inches to more than sixteen feet. Bridge clearance, minus towers and canvas tops, starts at six feet six inches and runs to about eight feet six inches. Weights go from forty-five hundred pounds to more than seventy thousand

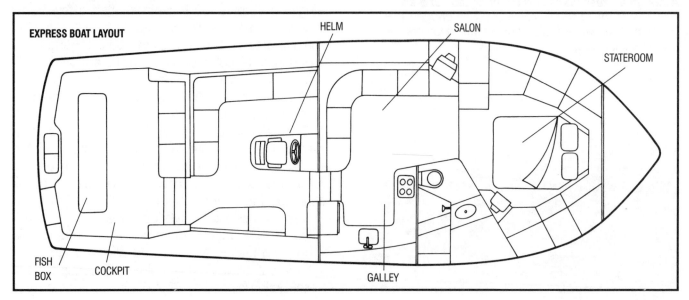

EXPRESS BOAT LAYOUT

HELM — SALON — STATEROOM

FISH BOX — COCKPIT — GALLEY

pounds on the extreme upper end. Drafts are two feet to four feet six inches.

Although primarily used as day boats, expresses are capable of making long, offshore runs. To provide them with range, fuel-tank capacities run from about one hundred gallons to four hundred gallons. Propulsion systems, either single installations on some boats less than thirty feet long and twin installations on bigger boats, start at about 250 horsepower and go well beyond the 1,000-horsepower mark. For expresses less than thirty feet long, top speed is usually in the high-40-mph range. For larger boats, the high 30s is an average top speed. Bottom configurations are typically deep-Vs and modified-V hulls. Prices for these hard-core fishing boats, which benefit in cost effectiveness by not being fitted with plush salons and deckhouses, start in the neighborhood of sixty thousand dollars and can run to more than a half million dollars for the largest rigs.

As noted, the main feature on an express is a long deck that accommodates both the aft cockpit and the helm. Features found in the cockpit are typical for large cabin boats and walkarounds. They include all the common items found on medium-to-large fishing boats, such as: storage compartments (including fish boxes, live wells, and coolers), rocket launchers, tackle drawers, full transoms (some with doors), tackle-preparation stations, fighting chairs, toe rails, under-gunwale rod racks, bolster pads for the coaming, and other offerings. Features found in the helm area are also typical for boats of this size. They include twin pedestal chairs or a bench seat, windshield, dash panels with splash covers, a wide array of electronic instruments, lockable boxes, side storage compartments, chart tables with plastic covers, overhead electronics boxes, and many other options.

Unlike engine compartments in convertibles, which are located in cramped quarters beneath the salon, expresses typically place the engines beneath the helm. To reach them, most expresses use hydraulic rams to lift a large portion of the deck. This arrangement leads to easy overhead access to all corners of the engine compartment.

As on other types of boats, expresses use the exterior structure of the cabin to mount antennae, outriggers, Bimini tops, sunshades, T-tops, hard tops, radar arches, and aluminum towers. Since expresses are big enough to accept substantial weight aloft and have relatively low centers of gravity, many are equipped with aluminum towers with hard tops and a second set of controls. On large expresses, tall tuna towers are fairly common. To increase foul-weather protection, many bridge decks are fitted with front and side curtains.

A companionway hatch between the two helm seats leads to the cabin area, which is located below the foredeck. Expresses typically sleep no more than four, although the largest boats may accommodate six. In boats less than thirty feet long, sleeping accommodations may be little more than forward V berths. In boats between thirty and forty feet, convertible berths (single or double) may be located in the dinette. In yachtlike expresses, staterooms are not uncommon.

Galleys, dinettes, and marine heads can be located either on the main deck or on a lower deck reachable by a forward hatch and steps. However, few of these areas approach the level of luxury found on typical convertibles, and frankly, most express owners find this one of the design's chief attributes. While expresses can run one hundred miles offshore and offer substantial creature comforts, they cost considerably less than convertibles of similar length. Regarding performance, express owners typically drive the boats themselves and find that the smaller profiles reduce windage and lower the center of gravity to diminish the tendency to rock and roll.

Although expresses aren't as specialized as center consoles, walkarounds, or convertibles, the compromise they've struck works well in both fishing and cruising layouts, both on saltwater and on large, freshwater lakes. For these reasons and many more, express boats are found in all parts of the country, and their popularity continues to climb.

DUAL CONSOLES

Another hybrid fishing rig that's found in all corners of the country and works well in both saltwater and freshwater environments is the **dual-console boat.** Like flats boats and center consoles, dual consoles are small boats intended to be fished by a crew of two to four. Their trademark is a split or walk-through console that takes its inspiration from the world of freshwater runabouts. Another trademark element is an open bow, similar to a freshwater bow rider. With this layout, it's easy to see how dual consoles can be easily pressed into use for waterskiing, joy riding, and other multiuse applications. As more people each year seek versatility and value for their money, the popularity of dual-console saltwater fishing boats continues to grow each year.

The size of the typical dual console runs from seventeen feet to twenty-three feet long. Beams range from seven feet to a bit more than eight feet. Drafts are from one foot to two feet. Weights are typically from one thousand pounds to just under three thousand pounds.

As small, open-bow boats, dual consoles are not intended for offshore running, but they are well suited to inshore and tidal conditions. As such, they are fitted with low freeboard, deep-V and modified-V hulls, and fuel tanks that hold between thirty and one hundred gallons. Propulsion systems are almost exclusively outboards (with a few sterndrives thrown in) and they deliver a power range in the neighborhood of 110 horsepower to 450 horsepower. Beginning at about twelve thousand dollars,

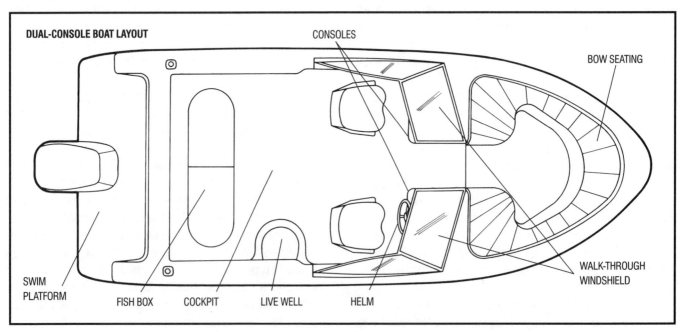

DUAL-CONSOLE BOAT LAYOUT

CONSOLES

BOW SEATING

SWIM PLATFORM

FISH BOX

COCKPIT

LIVE WELL

HELM

WALK-THROUGH WINDSHIELD

prices can reach as high as thirty thousand dollars with big dual-outboard installations.

As with freshwater bowriders, the placement of the dual-control consoles is well forward of amidships. This configuration creates a large, unified aft cockpit for a relatively small boat and doesn't split up the fishing area as does a center console. Boats of this type come with either cutout transoms and flip-up splashboards or full transoms and outboard brackets. Both configurations are common. Cockpit features are kept to a minimum, but they frequently include rocket launchers, toe rails, under-gunwale rod racks, gunwale-mounted outriggers, downriggers, live wells, fish boxes, coolers, and other equipment. Multiuse features include a swim platform or swim steps with a transom grab-rail and a fold-down ladder.

The appeal of having a split console, which is connected in the middle by a hinged windscreen, is protection from wind and spray. The traditional arrangement places the helm to starboard; a companion console is located to port. Both are faced by pedestal chairs. Like all helm consoles, these units are equipped with throttles, ignitions, dash panels, electronic instruments, glove boxes, storage compartments, and other familiar features. The companion console also have storage compartments, drink holders, radio/cassette players, and so forth.

Few dual-console boats are fitted with welded-aluminum T-tops or hard tops, although there are exceptions. Many, however, have Bimini tops or sunshades, and when equipped with side curtains, this turns dual-console rigs into good all-weather fishing platforms.

The bow area in most dual-console boats is a mini seating area that's rarely used in fishing scenarios, although it offers a good location in which to relax without getting in anyone's way. Some large, dual-console boats actually come with enclosed bows, which are occasionally fitted out like lean-and-mean cuddies.

For boaters who want an inshore, trailerable rig that can perform double duty for family entertaining and fishing, dual-console boats are an exercise in compromise that can do both.

ROLLED-EDGE AND OTHER SKIFFS

We all know what a skiff is—a small boat. The term is applied loosely to any simply constructed and outfitted small boat. Sailboats, powerboats, and rowboats can all be called skiffs. So, what's a **rolled-edge skiff**? It's a fiberglass skiff that's built without a top deck, which makes it relatively unique in modern boating. A single mold is used in this kind of boat, and every feature is built layer upon layer, including the bilge area, stringers, foam flotation, and deck features. Without a top deck, there are no distinctive gunwales. In their place are rolled edges, which are finished off by the addition of rub rails.

Boats like this, with minimal drafts, low profiles, and flat hulls, are sometimes referred to as bay boats, because they are generally used in protected coastal waters. As trailerable rigs, many are used on both fresh water and salt water, which makes them perfect choices for fishermen located along the tidal waters that stretch from Texas to the Carolinas.

As noted, rolled-edge skiffs are small boats, ranging from about fifteen feet to twenty-one feet. Beams run from six feet to roughly eight feet. Drafts are rarely more than a foot. Weights run from as little as seven hundred pounds to just under two thousand pounds.

Since these are trailerable boats and aren't intended to make long runs, fuel capacity ranges from six gallons to fifty gallons. Hull configurations are typically flat bottoms or shallow-Vs; however, some rigs feature a tunnel slot that channels water to a raised prop, which is ideal for skinny-water

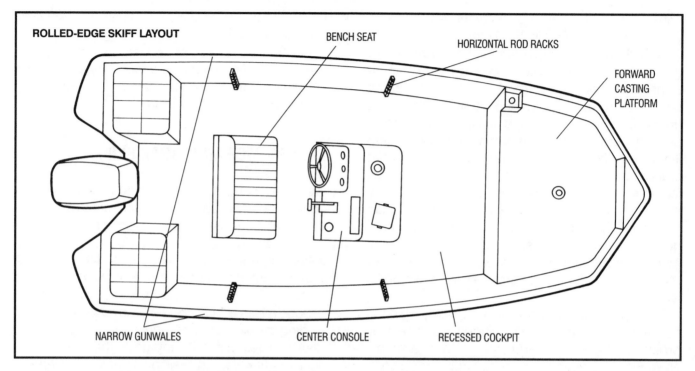

ROLLED-EDGE SKIFF LAYOUT

BENCH SEAT

HORIZONTAL ROD RACKS

FORWARD CASTING PLATFORM

NARROW GUNWALES

CENTER CONSOLE

RECESSED COCKPIT

conditions. The propulsion system of choice is a single outboard with a power range running from 40 horsepower to 200 horsepower. Tiller-handle outboards are common on smaller boats. Top speed is generally just under 50 mph, but some go faster. Prices run a wide gamut from less than ten thousand dollars (with motor) to double that amount.

Layout in a typical rolled-edge boat features a recessed cockpit with a raised forward casting platform and a starboard-mounted or center-mounted console. Common alternatives include raised fore and aft casting platforms and dual consoles. The cockpit sole is typically coated with a splatter-finish gel coat that's rough enough to provide traction without having a nonskid pattern. Dual-purpose bay boats come with marine carpeting.

Standard features are minimal on these affordable boats. They typically include a bench seat be-

hind the console, snap-on seat pads for the lids of storage compartments, horizontal rod racks, a dash panel with minimal instruments, a cooler, cleats, glove box, storage compartments below the console and raised casting decks, grab rails, and a windscreen. T-tops and spotting platforms are virtually unknown in these boats. Commonly added are rocket launchers, outboard jack plates, trolling motors, rod lockers, bait wells, pedestal seat mounts on the casting platforms, drink holders, fishing and navigation electronics, Bimini tops, sunshades, and many other options.

Naturally, not all saltwater fishing skiffs are the rolled-edge variety. Many coastal fishermen use wooden skiffs, aluminum skiffs, and two-piece molded-fiberglass skiffs. Most of the wooden and aluminum skiffs are small flat-bottom, semi-displacement rigs that are somewhat less outfitted than modern rolled-edge boats. They are also rarer. The top-deck finished skiff has a shallow-V or modified-V bottom. Based on a design popularly known as the Jersey sea skiff, these boats perform surprisingly well offshore, although they are primarily used on protected inshore waters.

PILOTHOUSE FISHING BOATS

Certainly one of the oldest designs in boating is the **pilothouse** boat, a small cuddy-cabin boat with a fully enclosed helm. Sometimes referred to as a workboat, pilothouse fishing boats take their inspiration from commercial fishing rigs that head offshore in all seasons and all conditions. To help protect these fishermen from foul weather, the helm area is fully enclosed. It also has more than six feet of standing headroom, a hard top, and solid walls. Most pilothouse boats use a sliding or hinged door to seal off the helm and create a wheelhouse. Other boats use a variant on this theme and keep the aft area open.

Along with the pilothouse itself, there are three other defining characteristics: protected perimeter decks, a forward cuddy cabin, and an upward-slop-ing sheer line. Like walkaround boats, pilothouse boats typically have one deck level that begins in the open aft cockpit and continues around the pilot-house to an open foredeck. Both the side decks and foredeck are protected by raised gunwales.

A simple cuddy cabin is often located forward of the pilothouse and is reachable by a companion-way hatch. Features and appointments are spartan on most pilothouse boats. They may include a small galley, convertible dinette, minimal head, and a V berth. Some pilothouse boats actually dispense with the cuddy altogether to maximize deck space.

The final essential element on a pilothouse boat is a contoured sheer line that starts low at the transom and rises toward the bow. In some cases, the sloping sheer line is quite sharp, and the bow is protected by a substantial freeboard to withstand head seas.

With their origins in utility and commercial fishing, it's not surprising that pilothouse boats are rarely the most fully outfitted rigs on the water. Such niceties as built-in tackle boxes, transom doors, and tackle-preparation stations are not common on these rigs. Neither are spotting platforms, raised flybridge control stations, or any type of welded aluminum tower.

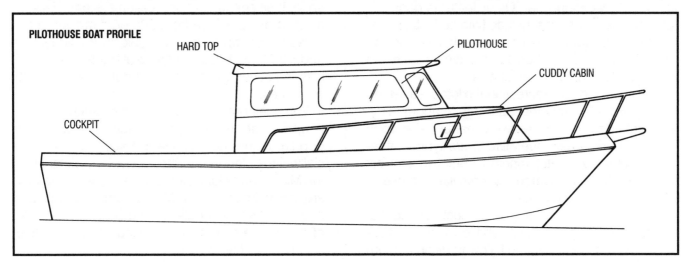

PILOTHOUSE BOAT PROFILE

HARD TOP · PILOTHOUSE · CUDDY CABIN · COCKPIT

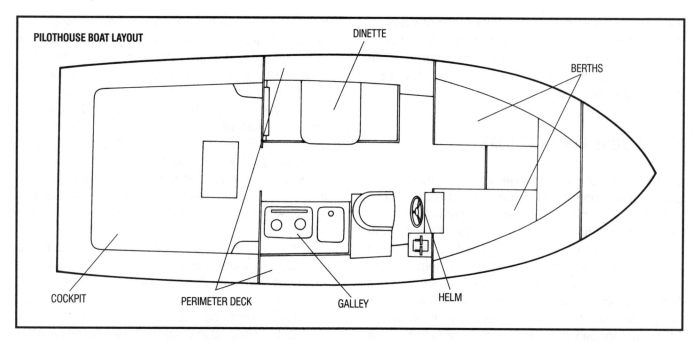

PILOTHOUSE BOAT LAYOUT

DINETTE

BERTHS

COCKPIT

PERIMETER DECK

GALLEY

HELM

Typical cockpit and deck features include rocket launchers, cleats, under-gunwale rod racks, bow pulpits, coolers, fish boxes, live wells, downriggers, and other essential items.

While the cockpit may be relatively bare, helm stations typically feature a full complement of operation and navigation gear. Other features generally found in the pilothouse include twin pedestal seats, overhead electronics boxes, storage boxes, coolers, drink holders, navigation tables, dinettes (in the larger boats), and other amenities.

The size range for recreational pilothouse fishing boats starts at twenty feet and runs to about thirty-five feet. Beams are relatively narrow—between eight feet and twelve feet. Drafts are typical of inboard-powered boats, ranging from two feet six inches to four feet. Weights are similar to those of walkaround and cabin boats.

While most modern pilothouse boats are configured with V bottoms (typically shallow-V or modified-V, plus a few deep-V), some follow tradition and are fitted with semidisplacement hulls. Inboard engines are the power of choice in large pilothouse boats, typically in twin-engine installations. Diesel engines are generally preferred over gas in boats like these. Outboards and sterndrives are seen on smaller boats. As a class, pilothouse boats are not renowned for their speed, and propulsion systems deliver a modest power range from 200 horsepower to 600 horsepower. Top speeds are typically no higher than about 35 mph. Prices for these utilitarian rigs start at less than twenty-five thousand dollars and run into six figures.

With their outstanding spray and weather protection, it's not surprising that pilothouse boats are popular along the cold-water Pacific Coast, especially in the Northwest. They are also popular along the Middle and North Atlantic Coast, where variants are sometimes called Maine boats, Down East boats, and lobster boats. On the Great Lakes, boats of this type are sometimes called salmon boats or simply Great Lakes boats.

FLYBRIDGE SPORTFISHERMEN

Notable for accommodating big-boat features on a modest-size hull, flybridge sportfishermen are one of saltwater fishing's most venerable designs. Appearing on all coasts and in all climes, versatile flybridge fishing boats fill a gap somewhere between express boats and convertibles, on one hand, and walkaround and cabin boats, on the other. Beginning at just twenty-five feet in length and running to about thirty-five feet, flybridges are notable for their large cockpits, raised bridge decks, and fully enclosed deckhouses with comfortable overnight accommodations.

The main feature that defines a flybridge boat is a modest-size bridge deck raised above an equally modest-size deckhouse. In small flybridge boats, this elevation can be just a handful of steps. In large boats, it can be a full story above the main deck. From here the captain has a lofty perch to aid navigation and survey the waters for signs of fish. Since these boats are generally smaller than convertibles and expresses, the bridge deck is simply outfitted with a control console, low windscreen, and either twin pedestal chairs or a single bench seat.

A second signature feature on a flybridge boat is a deckhouse. Comfortably protected from the weather and fitted with a modest salon, galley, and dinette, the deckhouse is an appealing amenity. But, unlike convertibles, flybridge boats rarely come with enclosed helm stations located on the main deck; however, some fishermen add a second helm on a spotting platform or short tower. Tall tuna towers are rarely found on flybridges, because few of these rigs can handle a great deal of weight aloft.

In many ways a flybridge boat may be called a lesser convertible, but this is unfair to the boat's clever achievement of squeezing so many features into a relatively small package. Fitting in with a theme of modest aspirations, the carpeted and air-conditioned salon typically offers a sitting area that converts into a dinette or extra berths, and little more. The galley, although functional, is far from plush. And the stateroom, which is located forward and a couple of steps below the main deck, typically consists of a double berth, closets, drawers, and a marine head.

Power of choice on flybridge boats is inboard engines. Twin-engine installations and diesel power plants are popular on most flybridges. The engine compartment is typically located beneath the salon and is accessed through a hatch in the cockpit. Cramped quarters for maintenance and repair duties are common.

Like other medium-size planing hulls, flybridges typically have modified-V and shallow-V bottoms. Drafts are similar to express boats and convertibles, but beams are narrower and weights slimmer. Power range for the propulsion systems is less, too. This adds up to a boat with modest pretensions and relatively affordable prices, equivalent to that of walkarounds and cabin boats when similarly outfitted.

There's no doubt that hybrid boats make up a large part of the saltwater fishing waterscape, and it would take a book in itself to cover the subject comprehensively. Comprising niche boats, regional designs, and custom or semicustom craft, hybrids are without question the most interesting and inventive segment in boating, and the arena where future classics are born.

CHAPTER 6

OUTFITTING: ELECTRONICS, EQUIPMENT, ACCESSORIES

Hemingway's fishing boat, *Pilar,* was relatively bare when it left the Wheeler Brothers' Bronx boatyard. Fishermen traditionally picked up their new boats this way: Only essential equipment was installed by the builder. Refinements were added by a rigging shop at a later date. In many ways, these boats were works in progress, and for a large number of fishermen, outfitting took place over a lifetime. Late in life, Hemingway actually commented to friends that he never felt he completed *Pilar,* even after owning her for three decades and adding numerous modifications. Like most anglers, he kept a mental list of improvements he intended to make as soon as time and money allowed.

To a certain extent, modern saltwater fishing boats are works in progress, too. However, dramatic changes in the building and marketing of boats have greatly affected outfitting in recent years. This is especially true in the past decade, when a trend known as the **package boat** took hold. Package

boats are manufacturer-rigged boats that arrive on the showroom floor fully outfitted and ready for launching—a complete reversal of boat-building tradition. In years past, virtually every component on a boat was sold separately and installed by a dealer, a process that often doubled the original asking price of a showroom boat.

Package boats, on the other hand, streamline both the buying and the outfitting process. Package boats often come fitted with a long list of standard equipment and are an alternative to buying a bare boat and then adding on so-called "options" (engines, seats, and other equipment you can't really do without). Many package boats are so well outfitted that they have only a few options available at the time of purchase. Some have none.

The package-boat trend has shifted some of the boat's outfitting process from the fisherman to the builder. And, to a certain extent, this isn't all bad. After all, builders know everything there is to know about a boat's specifications, construction, structure, and capabilities. By making outfitting decisions based on this knowledge, especially during the early design phase, manufacturers can integrate many features into the boat's structure. They can also perform the outfitting duties themselves—the wiring, plumbing, mounting, and so forth—and directly supervise the entire boat's quality control. This is important, because in a package boat, every feature will affect buyer satisfaction, a powerful motivating force that gives builders a vested interest in seeing that the rigging job is done right. A final positive spin on package boats: Manufacturers achieve economies of scale by making bulk purchases of equipment, and the savings is reflected in sticker prices that are frequently of outstanding value.

But manufacturers walk a fine line with package boats, especially on saltwater fishing boats. While some fishermen appreciate prerigging of engines, basic layout, and essential features, many still want to make a significant portion of outfitting decisions themselves. Another large bloc of fishermen simply want lean-and-mean boats without all the up-to-the-minute frills. The danger for the one-size-fits-all philosophy is that one man's fully rigged dream machine is sometimes another man's Edsel.

Still, in some form or other, the package-boat concept is here to stay. Not only is this true of smaller fishing boats—center consoles, flats boats, and walkarounds—where decision-making is limited by the size of the rig, but it's also true of express boats and convertibles, where the sky is sometimes the limit. An increasing number of new expresses and convertibles are now being prerigged with a long list of standard features and offered to buyers with only a choice of engines and nonessential features.

As mentioned in the last chapter on hybrid boat designs, several saltwater fishing-boat topics can fill entire books in themselves. Outfitting is certainly one of them. The following section, then, serves as a basic primer on accessories, equipment, and gear that are frequently used on modern saltwater fishing boats.

NAVIGATION ELECTRONICS

Marine electronics is a huge, specialized subject that is basically divided into three categories: navigation, fishing, and operation/safety. To most fishermen, it is further divided into two categories: necessities and luxuries. For the most part, this section will be devoted to necessities.

The most vital navigation instrument on a saltwater fisherman's dash is either a loran or a GPS receiver. These units answer a fisherman's most important question: Where am I? In addition to providing this answer with a high degree of accuracy, top-of-the-line units also do quite a bit more.

Loran is an acronym for *long range navigation*. The current loran-C system grew out of technology from World War II called loran-A, which has long since been supplanted. To access loran-C information, fishermen use a loran-C receiver, which is an electronic instrument that receives and interprets radio-navigation information on a frequency of 100 kHz. The unit receives pulsed signals that are continuously broadcast from a system of shore-based transmitters located along the United States and Canadian coastlines. In most areas, the signals can be received up to two hundred miles offshore. By measuring the difference in arrival time between the signals from a master and a secondary transmitter, a loran receiver can determine a boat's position. It displays its navigation information in numbers called LOPs (lines of position) or TDs (time differences). To perform these functions, a loran receiver requires an antenna, an accurate timer, and a minicomputer.

In addition to determining position, many loran units convert LOPs and TDs into latitude-longitude coordinates, which can be used to fix a boat's position on charts. Top-of-the-line units also calculate time, speed, and distance to destinations; plot courses; show course-deviation graphics; store individual waypoints and routes; sound alarms for arrival and cross-track error; interface with other electronic instruments at the helm; and perform many other navigation functions. However, from a fisherman's point of view, one of the greatest strengths offered by this equipment is its ability to direct your return to a previously logged location (a reef, wreck, buoy, and so forth) with pinpoint accuracy. If you've found a location where the fish are biting, you can record the TDs and be certain of returning to within a boat's length of the exact spot. This characteristic holds true when guided back by the loran that recorded the original TDs. Using a different unit will probably be somewhat less accurate.

Fortunately for inshore and nearshore fishermen, prices for loran units have fallen precipitously in recent years. A large part of the reason is that there's a

Using information transmitted from a minimum of four satellites, a GPS receiver can determine a boat's position in three dimensions: longitude, latitude, and altitude.

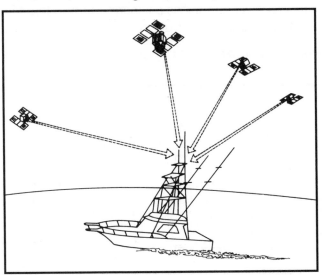

new kid on the radio-navigation block: the **GPS (Global Positioning Satellite)** system.

Originally developed by the United States Department of Defense in the 1980s to guide military aircraft, warships, and missiles, GPS is now the centerpiece of civilian navigation. In a nutshell, GPS is an exercise in triangulation involving a system of twenty-four satellites. Each satellite keeps track of where it is and what time it is, and transmits this information continuously to earth. A GPS unit picks up these data and compares the difference in time between when the information was sent and when it was received. Using these data to calculate the distance to at least three satellites (plus one more to double-check time), the GPS unit then triangulates to fix a position in three dimensions: longitude, latitude, and altitude.

Being a Pentagon-designed system, Global Positioning Satellites broadcast two different signals—one military and one civilian. The military signal is an encrypted code, and only American and allied military users carrying special equipment can unscramble it. This signal produces position-fixing accuracy to less than fifty feet. The second signal is specifically designed for civilian use, but fearing that hostile forces might use it to guide missiles against friendly targets, the Pentagon has muddied the civilian signal with pseudo-random noise called Selective Availability (SA). When SA isn't operational, marine GPS receivers can produce positioning-fixing accuracy to less than fifty feet. When SA is operational, marine GPS units are accurate to about three hundred feet.

However, a new system has recently been tested that improves GPS accuracy even when SA is operational. It's called **Differential GPS** or DGPS, and it's capable of producing position-fixing accuracy to within fifteen feet. In addition to receiving satellite data, Differential Beacon Receivers (DBRs) also receive position-correction signals transmitted on a

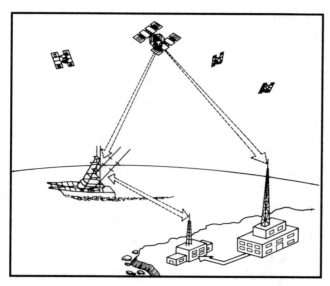

Using information transmitted from a land-based Differential Beacon, in addition to transmissions from satellites, a DGPS receiver can pinpoint locations to within a few feet.

different frequency by land-based units, currently in the prototype stage. Present plans call for the coast guard to operate Differential Beacons in major harbors by 1996. Complete coastal DGPS coverage is not yet planned.

Like loran units, GPS units (with or without DBRs)

can also calculate time, speed, and distance to destinations, plot courses, display course-deviation graphics, store individual waypoints and routes, sound alarms for arrival and cross-track error, interface with other electronic instruments at the helm, and perform many other navigation functions.

Regardless of the size of the boat, virtually all fishermen can take advantage of loran and GPS technology. In addition to being available as large-screen, fixed units, both types of receivers are now available in portable, handheld models.

A note about the future of loran: The government is currently committed to maintaining the loran-C system to the end of this century. After that time, continued funding and support is uncertain. The loran system has many fans, but most fishermen would probably be best advised to upgrade to the worldwide, interference-resistant coverage of GPS. To help fishermen make the transition, GPS sensor units are now available that provide existing equipment, such as lorans, fish-finders, radar, and plotters, with GPS capability. However, these sensors, which are basically antennae housings with built-in computers, cost nearly as much as a top-of-the-line GPS receiver. So unless a fisherman has a large investment already tied up in non-GPS electronics,

Especially useful in low-visibility situations, radar units send high-frequency radio transmissions and receive return echoes to determine what obstacles lie ahead.

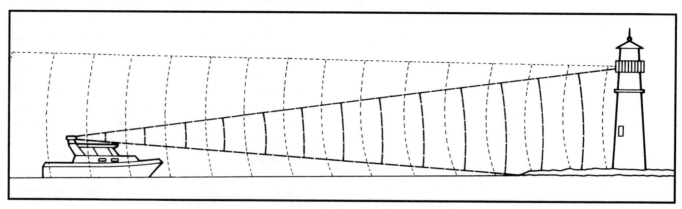

he'd probably be best advised to simply add a GPS receiver.

While loran and GPS units are ideal for both large and small fishing boats, **radar** (*r*adio *d*etection *a*nd *r*anging) was generally thought to be a big-boat feature. However, this situation is rapidly changing, and many boats as small as twenty-five feet in length are beginning to add radar to their helms. The beauty of radar is that in addition to providing range, bearing, speed, time to target, and other course information, it also offers a visual image of the boat's surroundings. Like highly sensitive electronic eyes, radar is extremely valuable during times of low visibility—storms, fog, and especially at night.

Unlike loran and GPS, radar isn't dependent

The two types of radar transmitting/receiving antennae: the radome, which is a compact, self-contained unit without external moving parts; and the wide-array antenna, which slowly rotates as it scans the horizon.

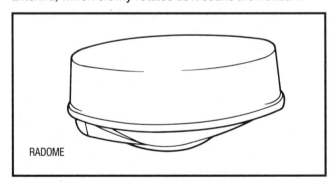

RADOME

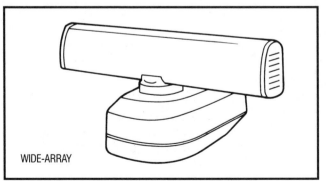

WIDE-ARRAY

upon receiving land-based or satellite signals. The radar unit itself transmits signals—pulsed high-frequency radio waves—and then collects the echoes that bounce back from distant objects. The time between transmission and the return echo is used to measure the distance to the object. In affordable radar units, the transmitter and receiver are combined in a fixed radome antenna. Larger boats typically use a rotating open-array antenna that delivers greater range and higher resolution.

While fishermen using small and medium-size boats would probably consider a chart plotter more of a luxury than a necessity, these units are becoming standard equipment on large boats. A **chart plotter** consists of a video display screen and high-powered computer that interfaces with other helm instruments, notably radar, depth-finders, GPS, and loran. High-end plotters often have GPS or loran capability built into the units themselves. A plotter's great strength is in providing real-time, highly readable course graphics. In addition, these units can store and display hundreds of waypoints, chart marks, and routes. A recent plotter enhancement is a disk-drive or cartridge-drive capability that gives the units an electronic library of highly detailed maps that can be used in addition to paper charts.

FISHING ELECTRONICS

The most important piece of fishing electronics on a typical helm is called a fish-finder, or more correctly a **depth-sounder**. These units use **sonar** (an acronym for *s*ound *n*avigation and *r*anging) technology to determine information about what's going on beneath the boat. This crucial information includes details of bottom structure and actual fish themselves.

With sonar, an electrical impulse is converted to a sound wave and transmitted into the water by means of a transducer mounted on the bottom of the hull. When the sound wave strikes an obstacle and bounces back, the time difference between the transmitted signal and the received echo is measured and the distance to the object is determined. The system is analogous to radar, except that sonar uses sound instead of radio waves.

The four most popular types of depth-sounders are known as flashers, paper recorders, liquid crystal displays (LCDs), and video sonars. **Flashers** are the simplest units. They get their name from a high-intensity neon bulb that rotates at a constant speed behind a display dial. The bulb lights up every time an echo is received, and this occurs so frequently, that the display appears nearly constantly lit. The location of the flickering light on the dial indicates the depth of the object causing the echo.

Many fishermen find that flashers have two drawbacks: They are hard to read in daylight, and they can't record data. Both of these problems have been solved by **chart recorders,** depth-sounders that record data on paper. While chart recorders solve some problems, they create others—notably a voracious appetite for expensive rolls of paper.

For a paperless depth-sounder, fishermen turn to **LCD recorders.** Information on an LCD recorder is displayed by means of a screen that uses liquid-crystal squares called pixels. By activating and de-activating pixels, the units draw a picture of the sonar information. Many units are equipped with such additional features as memory to play back recorded sequences, multiple depth ranges, water-temperature gauge, split-screen viewing, speed and route log, color display, and other capabilities.

Video depth-sounders are similar to LCD recorders except that they use cathode ray tubes (CRTs) instead of liquid-crystal display screens. The difference between the two is that CRTs are much

more sensitive to sonar signal intensity than LCD pixels. In addition to being able to display images in black and white, amber, or multiple colors, video depth-sounders can lock on to an area and display a constant view.

All four types of depth-sounder are available as permanently mounted base units or as portables. Many fishermen carry more than one depth-sounder aboard.

OPERATION/SAFETY ELECTRONICS

Even a seasoned skipper is put to the test on a day that starts out to be calm and suddenly turns blustery. The biggest fear is equipment failure. What happens when the going gets rough and a boat is dead in the water offshore? At times like this, a **VHF** (very high frequency) radio is a lifeline that connects the fisherman to other boats, marinas, weather channels, and the coast guard.

Because of potential distress scenarios, a VHF (technically referred to as VHF-FM) radio is a virtual requirement on all saltwater fishing boats. In fact, many fishermen carry multiple units when heading offshore: one twenty-five-watt base unit with a line-of-sight range of about twenty-five miles, and one

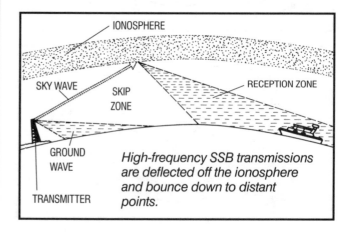

IONOSPHERE

SKY WAVE   SKIP ZONE   RECEPTION ZONE

GROUND WAVE

TRANSMITTER

High-frequency SSB transmissions are deflected off the ionosphere and bounce down to distant points.

portable handheld unit (with one to six watts of power) for backup.

Big-boat fishermen who go more than twenty-five miles offshore require **SSB** (single-sideband high seas) radiotelephones to maintain a communications lifeline. SSB radiotelephones transmit or receive radio frequencies that are bounced off the ionosphere. Communication by these units (typically ranging in power from fifty watts to one hundred fifty watts) is dependent upon many factors, such as the frequency used, atmospheric noise, interference, the time of day, sunspots, and other conditions. Depending on a combination of these factors, an SSB unit can have a range as short as fifty miles or as long as several thousand miles.

Both VHF radios and SSB radiotelephones require a ship-station license from the FCC. For more information on licensing, write to: Federal Communications Commission, Licensing Division, Consumer Assistance Branch, 1270 Fairfield Road, Gettysburg, PA 17325. Or call (717) 337-1212.

There are other communication links available to fishermen, but most of these are luxuries rather than necessities. They include: cellular phones (which can be useful to inshore and nearshore fishermen); CB (citizens band) radios; amateur or ham radios; and satellite phones that link up with COMSAT (Communications Satellite Corporation), which is the U.S. representative of INMARSAT (International Maritime Satellite Organization). Yachtlike fishing boats with large budgets frequently add the above equipment, but most fishermen can get by safely with VHF and SSB radios.

For fishermen who regularly go twenty miles or more offshore, an **EPIRB** (emergency *p*osition *i*ndi-cating *r*adio*b*eacon) unit is definitely not a luxury. When activated, an EPIRB transmits an emergency radio signal to a network of satellites. The coded sig-nal is transmitted continuously. It identifies the boat the EPIRB is on and pinpoints the location. For the signal to be useful in an emergency, the EPIRB must be registered with the FCC.

There are two basic types of EPIRBs, and they are differentiated by their transmission signals: EPIRBs that transmit on the 406-mHz frequency are Category I (defined by automatic activation and release when submerged in water) and Category II (defined by manual activation and release); EPIRBs that use the older 121.5-mHz and 243-mHz transmission signals are designated Class A (automatically activated and float free) and Class B (manual). Some high-end EPIRBs are equipped with radar transponders that emit radar echoes, which can be received by search-and-rescue radars to show the exact location of the EPIRB in relation to the search vessel or aircraft.

While not true necessities, two pieces of operational electronics also perform important safety roles—fuel-flow meters and autopilots. Fuel-flow meters provide fishermen with such crucial information as gallons per hour, miles per gallon, and total fuel burned. Such information can sometimes mean the difference between making it home or going dead in the water. In everyday use, fuel-flow meters help fishermen save money by maximizing their ability to achieve optimum fuel efficiency.

Equally useful is an autopilot, which enables fishermen to steer either by remote control or to set an automatically followed route. Autopilots work by connecting electric motors to either hydraulic or mechanical steering systems, or by replacing the steering control mechanism itself. In shorthanded fishing situations, autopilots can provide welcome relief to a small crew. In everyday use, the units can be programmed to execute carefully selected trolling patterns and, when interfaced with other helm instruments, accurately navigate during extended difficult conditions.

EQUIPMENT, ACCESSORIES, GEAR

So many products and so little time! Here is a limited list of items that many fishermen would probably consider necessities.

- Aluminum towers, which provide shelter and a raised vantage point to seek out fish, are generally found on large and medium-size boats. Small rigs may simply use a T-top (for a center console) or a hard top (for a cuddy). Some of these will be equipped with spotting platforms. Many will have a second set of controls. Larger boats (expresses and convertibles) typically opt for tall marlin towers or multistory tuna towers. Radar arches are less popular add-ons.
- Bait freezers and refrigerated fish boxes (some with macerator pumps) are typical big-boat features.
- Battery chargers perform the all-important task of keeping engine-cranking batteries fully charged. Large expresses and convertibles often keep a charger onboard. Other fishermen keep the units at home.
- Brackets for outboards are increasingly being integrated into boat molds, but when they aren't, many fishermen add bolt-on units to their transoms. Brackets enable boats to run with full transoms, as opposed to low, outboard cutaways. They also move the engines a few feet away from the fish-fighting area to allow greater freedom of movement with a fish on the line and add buoyancy to the transom area to allow the use of larger engines.
- Compasses are available either in traditional magnetic format (with floating pointers) or in a fluxgate format, which uses an electronic sensor to determine the direction of magnetic north. No fishing boat should be without one.
- Curtains, either front, side, or full enclosures, turn small and medium-size fishing boats into all-weather platforms.

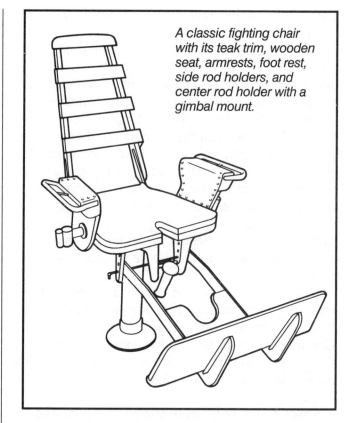

A classic fighting chair with its teak trim, wooden seat, armrests, foot rest, side rod holders, and center rod holder with a gimbal mount.

- Downriggers, usually provided in pairs mounted on opposite gunwales near the stern, are standard equipment for deep-trolling fishermen, especially those after kingfish on the East Coast and salmon on the West.
- Fighting chairs were originally developed with big boats in mind; however, many fishermen use them in medium-size walkarounds and center consoles, where they can be mounted either forward or aft. A fighting chair is equipped with a footrest, a gimbal-mounted rod holder, and a safety harness.
- Fire-extinguisher systems are standard equipment on large and medium-size boats, especially with inboard power. Many smaller inboard and sterndrive boats add them later.

- Gasoline vapor and CO_2 (carbon monoxide) detectors are also frequent additions to inboard and sterndrive-powered boats.
- Inverters—electric units that convert DC current to AC—are common big-boat features.
- Isolated battery systems are becoming standard items on boats that do a lot of trolling and have a number of electronic instruments. In this system, separate alternator outputs are used for each battery, which allows fishermen to dedicate one or more batteries to run accessories. Fishermen with this system can use their electronics all day without fear of running down the engine-cranking battery.
- Lights, either halogen or fluorescent, are mounted to towers and hard tops on boats that frequently go out at night.
- Live wells or bait wells are generally installed by boat builders, but most fishermen require more than a simple water-holding compartment. They also want recirculating pumps and aerators, which enrich the water with oxygen. These fea-

Beneath a hatch lid, a round-cornered bait well is equipped with deeply recessed gully drains, a waterpump, and an aerator.

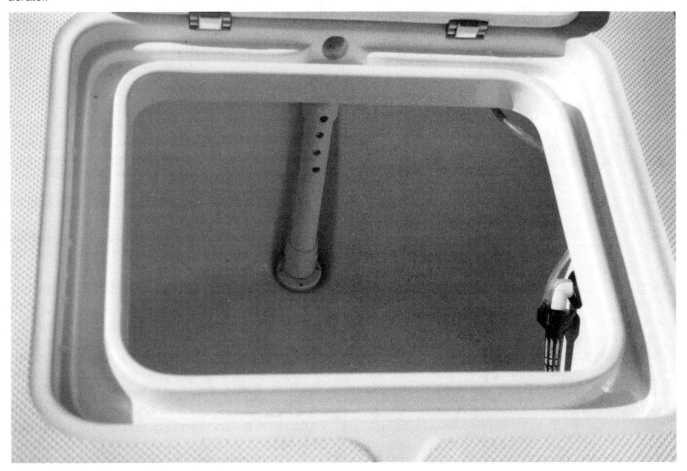

tures can be added to existing live wells or, as an alternative, fully equipped portable live wells can be brought on board.

- Outriggers are standard add-on features on all large and medium-size rigs. They are often installed as part of an aluminum tower. Some small-boat fishermen use gunwale-mounted or T-top-mounted outriggers. The purpose of outrigger poles and their halyards is threefold: to spread and separate multiple baits and lures; to provide an automatic drop-back of slack line when the cleat or rubber band pops off the halyard; and to lift the angle of each rod tip so that a minimal amount of line drags in the water.
- Padded-coaming bolsters are a welcome addition for bottom-fish anglers, who spend much of their time braced against the gunwales as they drift bait.
- Pedestal seats, originally found on freshwater bass boats, are increasingly being added to center consoles, flats boats, and skiffs.
- Rocket launchers, or vertical rod holders, are frequently preinstalled by builders in gunwales and other locations. However, many fishermen believe that a boat can't hold too many rods, so they add them to the transom, base of a center console, back of a leaning post, back of a T-top or hard top, and to the aft railing of a raised bridge. Some holders have pivoting rod mounts that allow setting the hook while the rod is still in the holder, although this is not a recognized method for catching record fish.
- Rod racks are usually built into the bulwarks beneath the gunwales, and few fishermen are required to add them here. However, on enclosed-deck boats that go out with sizable crews, horizontal rod racks are frequently installed in cabins and salons. Vertical rod racks are common alongside center consoles.
- Shore-power hookup allows batteries to be

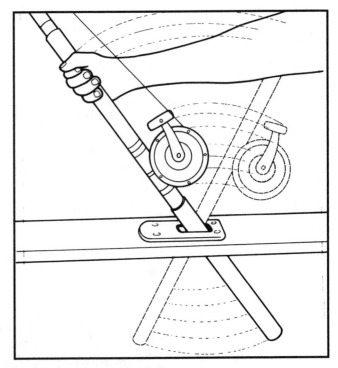

A pivoting rod holder enables fishermen to set the hook while the rod is still in the rocket launcher. Record catches boated this way, however, are disallowed.

charged and the bait wells to run all night without draining onboard batteries.

- Sunshades and Bimini tops are virtual necessities for boats without towers and enclosed helms.
- Tackle drawers and tackle-preparation stations are typically integrated by the boat builder. When they aren't, fishermen can get them installed.
- Trim tabs are increasingly being included as standard equipment. Once considered strictly a big-boat feature, trim tabs are now popular on boats smaller than twenty feet in length.
- Trolling motors (electric) are also a bass-boat innovation enjoying widespread popularity on flats boats and skiffs.
- Water-temperature gauges are often included as

a feature on top-of-the-line fish-finders. When they aren't, fishermen frequently add stand-alone units.

- Windlasses, or anchor winches mounted on bow pulpits, are virtually standard equipment on large boats. Deep-water bottom fishermen on medium-size boats often include them in their rigging package.

CHAPTER 7

BOAT HANDLING AND MAINTENANCE

Part 1-Boat Handling

What's the minimum knowledge required to run a boat offshore and maintain it? The short answer is none. There is no minimum. Saltwater fishermen can't know too much about these important subjects. But if there were a definable minimum and if the information were collected, bound, and published, it would probably look something like *Chapman Piloting* (Hearst Marine Books, William Morrow and Company, 1350 Avenue of the Americas, New York, NY 10019). *Chapman* is the recognized authority in boating, and reading it is a recommended starting point for all boaters.

However, despite its six-hundred-plus, large-format pages, *Chapman* is a generalist's book. Fishermen, especially saltwater anglers, require a specialized body of knowledge that goes beyond basic seamanship, the rules of the road, navigation, coast guard regulations, equipment operation, and dealing with emergencies. Saltwater anglers need to know boat-handling techniques that help them hook and boat fish. They also need to know all about keeping their boat, typically the second largest investment made by its owner, in tip-top shape. And this is no mean feat, considering that the ocean is one of the most hostile and corrosive environments on the planet.

Here then are tips and techniques aimed specifically at saltwater angling, starting first with the basics of boat handling.

ANCHORING

While most fishermen think of anchoring as a technique used to catch bottom fish in relatively shallow waters, the technique is also used by experienced captains in five-hundred-foot to seven-hundred-foot canyons. To accomplish this technically difficult feat

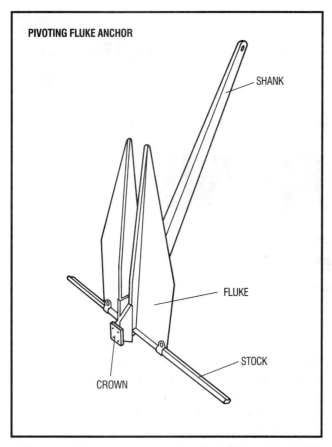

PIVOTING FLUKE ANCHOR

SHANK

FLUKE

STOCK

CROWN

requires a sound knowledge of anchoring basics, which can serve anglers well in all situations.

To achieve 100-percent holding power, the textbook recommendation for **scope ratio** (the length of anchor line in relation to depth of the water) is about 7:1. In twenty feet of water, this means an anchor line (rode plus chain) of one hundred forty feet. Using this scope ratio, the angle of pull is low and the anchor's hold on the bottom is secure. Using less line or scope increases the angle of pull and decreases the anchor's holding power.

While a 7:1 scope ratio may be realistic for relatively shallow-water fishing, such as reefs, flats, inlets, passes, and other inshore features, it becomes a major burden at depths of five hundred feet to seven hundred feet. Here, the recommended scope ratio would require anchor line between thirty-five hundred and forty-nine hundred feet. For this reason, many fishermen (and general boaters, too) typically reduce the scope ratio to somewhere around 4:1, and find that it works well in all but the worst conditions. But even this reduced ratio means lines of between two thousand and twenty-eight hundred feet in deep-water canyons.

One good tip to help reduce this line requirement

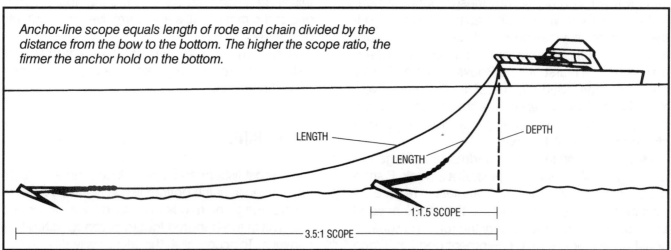

Anchor-line scope equals length of rode and chain divided by the distance from the bow to the bottom. The higher the scope ratio, the firmer the anchor hold on the bottom.

DEPTH

LENGTH

LENGTH

1:1.5 SCOPE

3.5:1 SCOPE

is to increase the weight of the chain, either by doubling the length from about fifteen feet to thirty feet or by switching to heavier chain. The increased weight will pull the line nearest the anchor farther down to the bottom, which creates a more favorable angle of penetration for the anchor. For this technique to work, the captain has to lower the anchor very slowly, taking care not to allow the chain to fall quicker than the anchor, and wrap around it on the way down. Captains can typically get away with scopes below 3:1 by using this technique.

Once the captain has mastered deep-water anchoring, the next big chore is anchor retrieval. To make this tricky process go more smoothly, many captains employ a technique that involves a floating inflatable ball. This ball is used to increase the angle of rode (thereby reducing the anchor's holding power) and then float it to the surface, where a crewman can easily pull it in.

The setup includes an inflatable mooring ball, several feet of rope, a snap shackle, and a customized stainless-steel ring that has a lockable opening. When the time comes to raise the anchor,

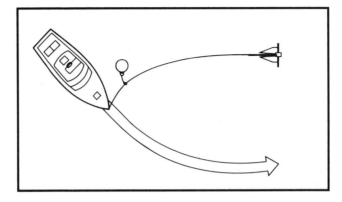

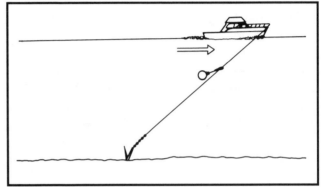

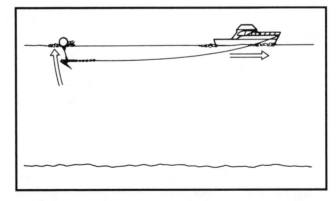

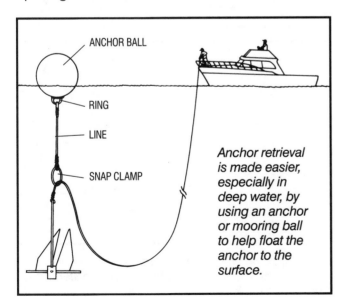

ANCHOR BALL

RING

LINE

SNAP CLAMP

Anchor retrieval is made easier, especially in deep water, by using an anchor or mooring ball to help float the anchor to the surface.

The first steps in using an anchor ball are to close the stainless-steel ring around the anchor line and toss the ball overboard. Then run the boat around the ball in a wide circle to loosen the anchor from the bottom without damaging it. Finally, run the boat ahead until the anchor makes contact with the ball and drags it beneath the surface. At this point, winching effort is greatly reduced.

you must put the anchor rode through the stainless-steel ring, lock it tight, and then toss the mooring ball overboard. Now start the engines and run the boat in a wide circle around the ball until the increasing angle of rode and pressure on the line dislodges the anchor. Then increase boat speed and pull the rode through the stainless-steel ring. The resistance of the water will hold the ball still enough in place. When the chain engages the ring, the mooring ball will submerge. At this point, the anchor is virtually on the surface, and the rode can be easily retrieved.

One final tip: Deployment and retrieval of the anchor in these deep-water locations can be time-consuming. If the need arises to move quickly, either to chase a fish or to get out of the way of a passing freighter, the hauling-up process can become a major problem. To solve it, experienced fishermen tie a float to the end of the anchor line and toss it overboard when quick movement is required. You can always go back to retrieve it at a later time.

TROLLING

Trolling is without doubt the most popular technique used for offshore fishing. It's done from a slowly moving boat that trails a pattern of lures or bait. It not only enables fishermen to cover a sizable area of water for bait presentation, but if executed properly, it draws fish right to the boat.

Although trolling appears to be a relatively straightforward procedure, there are numerous strategies. Many are played out by the crew handling the bait (these include rod and line selection, bait and lure patterns, downrigger depths, bait/lure combinations, and other methods). Many other strategies are played out by the captain driving the boat. Let's concentrate on the latter.

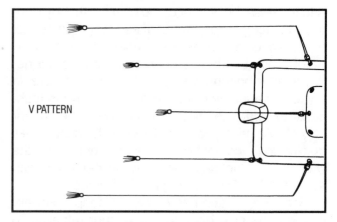

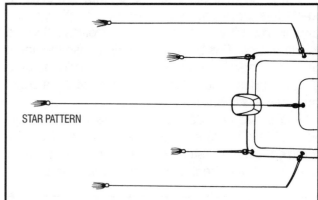

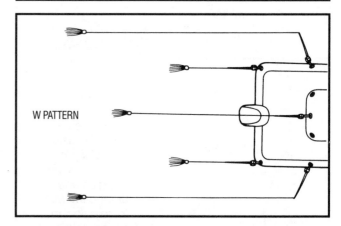

The most common trolling patterns can be used for either natural or artificial bait. They are the V pattern, star pattern, and the W pattern.

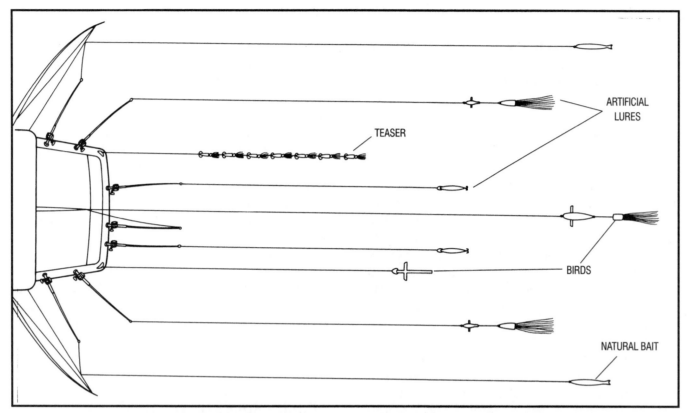

ARTIFICIAL
LURES

TEASER

BIRDS

NATURAL BAIT

A complex seven-line trolling pattern may include both natural and artificial bait and a host of additional attractants.

As far as the skipper is concerned, his primary duties are to prevent tangles from occurring in the bait pattern, spot and direct the crew to remove these tangles should they occur, make sure the baits ride properly through the water for optimum presentation, watch for signs of fish, and when a fish strikes, react with an intelligent battle plan.

Of all the decisions the captain must make while trolling, speed is probably the most crucial. This decision is based on the following four factors: size or type of boat; water conditions; type of bait being used; and targeted fish.

Wake characteristics are an important factor in determining trolling speed, and this is codependent on the size or type of boat. Ideally, the baits should be running in clear water, as opposed to prop wash or hard wakes. The captain must adjust the throttle setting until the wakes are quartering off to the sides of the boat and away from bait pattern. In addition to monitoring turbulence, the captain must observe wave height and duration to see how they affect the presentation of the baits as they run through the water.

Artificial lures work best when they run right at the surface and create a smoky trail of turbulence in their wake. Natural baits work best when they run just below the surface. Neither is at its optimum when skipping along the crests of waves. In general, artificial lures can be run faster than natural bait, which loses freshness quickly when pulled too fast.

One final tip: If your target is fast-swimming bill-fish, then speeds up to fifteen knots have been known to induce trophy strikes. However, depending on the above factors, typical trolling speeds are in the five-knot to ten-knot range.

FISH-FIGHTING BATTLE PLAN

When a fish strikes a bait, many fishermen throw the engines into neutral, pull in the remaining lines, and then back down on the fish while yelling at the angler to keep the pressure on by reeling in line. Top tournament captains often use a different method, which recognizes a fact of fishing life: Game fish frequently run in small groups, and second and third fish sometimes feed when the first fish strikes. By pulling in the other lines, a captain eliminates the possibility of achieving one of fishing's most exciting moments—a multiple hookup.

Instead of throwing the engines into neutral, the captain with a hookup should do three things: maintain trolling speed (some actually speed up); determine the direction the fish is charging; and then turn in toward the fish. During this initial stage, only the rods on the inside of the turn need to be pulled and moved to the opposite side. To prevent the lines from tangling, rods may have to be passed over or under the line with the fish. Although this strategy requires quick effort and teamwork, the point is that once the crew pulls all the lines out of the water, the boat stops fishing. This doesn't have to be the case. In fact, if the fight is progressing well and the hooked fish isn't a giant tuna, shark, or marlin, the crew can actually let out fresh bait on the other lines.

Note that a skilled tournament captain turns in toward the fish after the hookup is made instead of backing down. This is the preferred boat-handling strategy, because a gamefish can swim faster than any boat can run in reverse. A boat is performing at its best when going forward, and this is true even when fighting a hooked fish. Once the captain has turned in toward the fish, he keeps it off to the side of the boat, where the angler faces the fish off one of the cockpit corners. During this phase, both the captain and the angler make sure that the line forms a minimum of belly in the water. The angler's job is to keep tension tight on the line. The captain can help by pivoting in place or by making tight turns instead of wide ones. In addition, when the fish makes a high-speed run, don't run ahead of the fish and unnecessarily strip off line. Stripped-off line can come back to haunt you when a belly forms or when the fish unexpectedly makes a final, desperate run.

In general, the time to back down on a fish is not when it is green and charging. The time to back down is when the fish stops or is in the process of being brought to boat. One exception might occur when an angler is threatened with running out of line. In this scenario, a captain has few options and may be forced to back down until enough line is retrieved.

FISHING RULES OF THE ROAD

"How would you feel if it happened to you?" Basically this is the question all captains must ask themselves when making decisions during boat-to-boat fishing encounters.

A good tip for hard-charging expresses or convertibles that cross paths with small fishing rigs is to back off the throttle or swing wide around them. It's no secret that big wakes cause problems for small boats, especially if they're anchored. Big boats, naturally, can handle large wakes without problems, but when they're anchored or drifting, they don't necessarily appreciate them either.

All boats, either large or small, should slow down or swing wide around a concentration of rigs that are working a hot fishing spot. Either carefully thread through the group at slow speed, or swing wide around it. Never roar through the middle of a concentrated group, even if there appears to be room. Anchor lines may be out, kites may be flying, fish may be on the hook. Even if a hard-charging boat doesn't strike equipment or swamp a boat, it might spook wary fish. Avoid causing these unnecessary problems whenever possible.

As a rule of thumb, a boat with a fish on the hook always has the right of way. As soon as a captain sees a nearby strike, he should immediately move out of the potential playing field.

When boats gather around bottom structure, the first boat at the spot has the right of way. Subsequent arrivals should approach cautiously and then maintain a reasonable distance. This is especially true when fishing in shallow water where gamefish spook easily.

Another general rule is to be considerate of an active chum line. Always run around it if possible, and maintain a reasonable distance. Tapping into a chum line is always inappropriate. Another guideline that applies to either chumming or fishing bottom structure: When you've caught your limit, give up your position to another angler.

A similar situation occurs when one boat discovers a school of gamefish and other boats move in to take advantage. The late-arriving boats should keep their distance from the main school and attempt to fish off the fringes. Certainly, a charge right to the middle of the school is inappropriate. First of all, the initial boat has the right-of-way, and second, the charging boat risks sending the schooling fish to the bottom.

GENERAL BOAT-HANDLING TIPS

Backing down on a fish means shifting into reverse during battle with a hooked fish. Since boats don't perform well in reverse, most of the battle should be conducted with the boat moving forward or pivoting in place to keep the fish off the cockpit corners. Backing down is recommended only in short bursts (as opposed to running mile after mile). It's appropriate when bringing fish to the boat during the end game or when loss of line is a serious problem. When backing down, the captain should keep a close watch on the rate of line retrieval to make sure that constant pressure on the fish is maintained. To prevent overrunning the line, most captains typically engage a single engine. Two other backing-down tips are to raise the trim tabs to prevent the planes from snapping off, and to keep a close eye on sea conditions to determine the throttle setting. Go very slowly in building seas, and avoid backing down entirely in high seas. A rogue wave coming in over the transom can swamp even the largest boat.

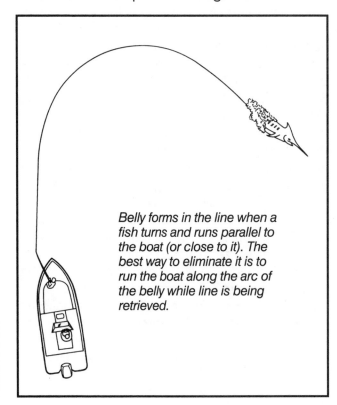

Belly forms in the line when a fish turns and runs parallel to the boat (or close to it). The best way to eliminate it is to run the boat along the arc of the belly while line is being retrieved.

Belly occurs in a line when a fish makes a hard charge and then changes direction before the line can be retrieved. Managing the belly is an important responsibility for the captain, because it greatly increases pressure on the line and makes imminent snapping off a real threat. To avoid snapping off, the captain should either run along the belly (tracing the curve with the boat) as the angler retrieves line, or run to the belly but not over it. While running to the belly, the angler sets the reel in freespool. Once the boat is near the belly, the angler resets the drag and eliminates the belly. The one situation a captain wants to avoid is running parallel to the fish and pulling the belly through the water. This maximizes pressure on the line and is a perfect recipe for a snap-off.

Chumming is done with finely chopped or ground particles of fish trailed in the water behind the boat. The goal is to use the scent of food to lure hungry gamefish toward the boat, which is done by tying a plastic jug or canister of ground bait off the boat at the transom. Chumming can be done while a boat is being poled, drifting, or trolling. If trolling, a slow speed (about two knots) works best. The best chum is made of the freshest bait. To get started in the morning, many fishermen use a solid block of frozen chum that they buy or make themselves using fish oil, cat food, dog food, scraps, and so forth. Chunking is similar to chumming, except that chunks of bait are added to the ground-fish particles. The theory is that larger gamefish are more attracted to bite-size food than to tiny particles.

Deep jigging or vertical jigging is a technique that allows anglers to fish a complete column of water from the bottom to the surface. The technique works in depths from thirty feet to three hundred feet. After arriving at the targeted area—either a reef, drop-off, canyon, or wreck—the captain can either drift with a favorable wind/tide or drop anchor. When drifting, it's important to keep a close eye on the depth-sounder. Whenever the boat drifts beyond the target zone, start the engine and idle back to a starting point. Then repeat the process. Naturally, it makes sense to begin drifting from an upwind/upcurrent starting point. The same is true when anchoring. When wind and current aren't favorable, trolling at very slow speeds is a good option.

Flats fishing, with either a flats boat, a skiff, or a low-freeboard center console, need not be confined to the Florida coast. It can be used on any tidal shallows, even in Maine or Alaska. The technique involves shutting down the engine and pushing the boat (by using either a pole or an electric trolling motor) into clear water that's two feet to five feet deep. Wearing polarized sunglasses, anglers scan the water for fish. When a fish is spotted, the proper procedure is to cast a lure, bait, or fly in front of the fish. If you're lucky, the fish will intercept it. If not, keep pushing and scouting.

Kite fishing is an ancient fishing technique refined in recent years by a Florida fisherman, Captain Bob Lewis, of Miami. The technique involves flying a kite off the transom to present bait at a distance from the boat to avoid spooking wary fish. It also keeps

Kite fishing is all about presentation. Wary fish are fooled because they don't see the leader or line—plus, the boat is far in the distance and the bait is kept dancing on the surface. All of this adds up to a successful trolling or drifting method.

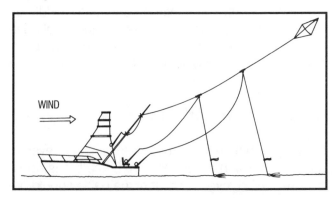

the bait on the surface of the water and presents it to the fish with line and leader invisible to the fish. Under ideal conditions, skilled captains can fly two or three kites. The kite-fishing setup includes a kite, kite rod and reel, and a kite line spliced with swivels and release clips. Many fishermen use an electric reel on the kite rod to more easily manage the line. Before letting out the kite line, the crew runs line from the fishing rods through the release clips. When the kite is flying, the bow of the boat should be kept into the wind or close to it. However, turns can be made across the wind to keep within the targeted fishing grounds. Either boats can be slow-trolled flying a kite or, if the wind is strong enough, allow the kite to pull the boat. Although the technique is especially effective for sailfish, it also works for other gamefish.

A final tip: Setting the hook is done by the fisherman holding the rod, but the boat captain can help. When a fish strikes a bait, the captain shouldn't stop or slow down the boat. Keep moving at the same trolling speed and help the angler stretch out the line to bend the rod with tension. This will increase hook penetration and quicken the initial pressure on the fish.

Part 2-Saltwater Maintenance

There are two primary reasons why saltwater anglers need to know all they can about boat/engine maintenance and repair. The first is that after displaying great skill in landing a trophy fish, the captain and crew share a fervent desire to get back to the marina in one piece. The second reason is that having committed a significant portion of one's present and future earnings toward the purchase of an expensive rig, a fisherman has a vested interest in making sure it remains seaworthy for at least as long as the payment schedule lasts, and hopefully, longer.

These are powerful motivators, and they inspire fishermen to study their boat and engine operation manuals as closely as possible. Manufacturer-supplied manuals like these provide fishermen with service-cycle recommendations, adjustment and repair tips, pre- and post-trip inspection procedures, and general guidelines and checklists that become the foundation of a rig's basic care and feeding over the long term.

In addition to these basics, there are a number of other tips and techniques that are specific to the saltwater environment and to fishing boats. These include the following:

- Batteries require clean terminal posts to pass an efficient current. Disconnect and scrape corrosion off with a wire brush or steel wool. It's also a good idea to check terminals periodically for tight connections and to spray with a corrosion retardant. For batteries that require maintenance, top off cells with distilled water and charge to the manufacturer's recommended specific gravity.

- Belts are subject to heavy wear and require frequent inspection for cracking, fraying, and the maintenance of proper tension. Always make sure you have replacement belts aboard. A general rule of thumb is that most belts have a four-year life cycle and should be replaced at this point as a preemptive procedure.

- Bilge areas need to be inspected on a regular basis. Look for solid mountings for all pumps, wires, hoses, and so forth. Clean drainages of all obstructions and debris. Check the seacocks and the through-hull fittings for solid seals. Check for excessive water or unusual oil and gas stains. Take corrective measures if necessary.

- Bottom scrubbing is important for large boats that live permanently in the water and should be done at least once a year depending on location to rid the boat of algae, barnacles, and other fast-growing parasites. The problem with bottom buildup is that it can pit the hull and, in worst-case scenarios, reduce running performance to the point where the boat plows through the water. The solution is to haul the boat out of the water to pressure wash and scrub the bottom. This is also the time to apply a new coat of antifouling bottom paint, although many fishermen alternate years between coats.

- Canvas covers can be obtained for virtually every part of the boat, and no fisherman owns too many of them. Constant sunlight is nearly as debilitating as salt spray over a long period of time. The combination of the two can be a disaster. Console covers are recommended for smaller boats, such as center consoles and skiffs. Cockpit and helm-station covers are recommended for walkarounds and cuddies. Express boats and convertibles benefit by covering the bridges and cockpits. Rather than cover these areas entirely, some boaters simply cover individual components, such as helm consoles, fighting chairs, spotting-platform control stations, windlasses, outboard motors, sterndrive outdrives, and so forth.

- Electrical outlets, both inside and outside the boat, benefit by the application of moisture-displacing lubricant.

- Freshwater washdown of all exposed surfaces should be standard procedure after every saltwater trip. Hook up a hose at a marina or a launch ramp and spray the boat top to bottom, forward and aft. This should include all outriggers, downriggers, rods, reels, gaffs, hardware, lines, anchors, antennae, canvas tops, and curtain enclosures. Basically, wash down everything that's been touched by salt water to ward off corrosion and staining. To ensure that the boat stays free of embedded dirt streaks and stains, wash them down immediately, even before the trip is complete. To conserve fresh water, a saltwater spray will do the job until the boat reaches the marina.

Everyone knows that gasoline or diesel fuel is toxic, but few know how to start a siphon without placing themselves in danger. A safe method is to insert a length of hose into the fuel can and allow it to fill up with fuel. Then squeeze off one end of the hose and draw it out of the can. When this end is below the can and aimed down at the fuel fill, release the hose and start the siphon.

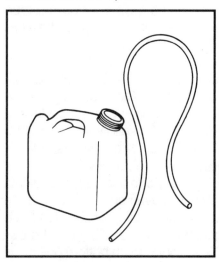 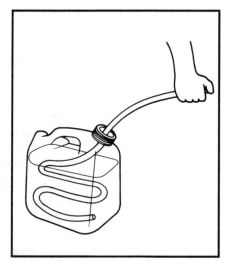 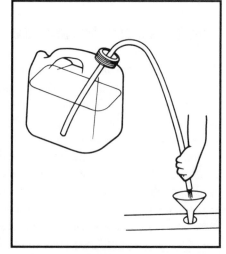

- Fuel containers are sometimes used by fishermen who head out to locations that are either on the fringes of a boat's running range or beyond it. The first rule of thumb is that no boat should attempt this alone. There is safety in numbers in case the fuel estimate turns out to be incorrect. A second rule of thumb—and a coast guard requirement—is to use only containers approved by the Department of Transportation. A third rule of thumb is to use plastic containers rather than metal ones, which may bang around and damage the cockpit. Large plastic bladders should be avoided, since they are subject to breaking a seam in rough seas. A fourth rule of thumb is to secure the containers as tightly as possible and make constant visual checks of the tie-downs during the course of the trip. Some general tips include: Use several smaller containers as opposed to one hard-to-handle large container; pump the fuel rather than pour it; and, if siphoning is required, never activate the siphon by using your mouth. A better method is to bring along a hose that's at least three times as long as the height of the container. Insert the hose into the container and then pinch off the open end with your thumb. With the hose filled with fuel and the air pinched off by your thumb, pull the hose out of the container and aim it down to the fuel fill. Release your thumb and the fuel should begin flowing.

- Gel-coat care starts with simple cleaning, polishing, and waxing, and then moves up to the more complex task of repairing cracks, gouges, and dings. The best way to keep the bloom on your gel coat is to remove surface dirt regularly and apply a cleaner/wax compound about once a month. This will protect against fading and chalking caused by ultraviolet light. Treat gouges and dings, even hairline spiderweb cracks, as soon as possible. Even the slightest cracks may ultimately allow water to seep between the laminates and into the coring. Clean out the surrounding area of chipped, cracked, and weakened gel coat and fiberglass. Then apply fiberglass filler from a kit closely following the directions. After the filler cures, sand it with coarse sandpaper to a level slightly lower than the surrounding surface. Now apply a layer of gel coat and let it cure. Finish this off with sandpaper and layers of polish and wax.

- Hardware that's stout and of good quality should last the lifetime of a boat, even if it's peeling, pitted, or stained. However, if aesthetics are a concern, peeling chrome can be replated at a shop that specializes in electroplating. Pitting and rust stains are sometimes the result of impurities left behind in the manufacturing process. Simply scrape off the rust and treat the area with a metal cleaner/polish. All hardware benefits by the regular application of moisture-displacing lubricants and a coat of wax.

- Spare parts are an important addition to every boat because most offshore fishing spots are far from the nearest marine chandlery and, unfortunately, they don't deliver. A short list of vital spare parts includes: engine belts, hoses, hose clamps, fuses, wire, wire-crimp fittings, oil, oil filters, fuel/water separators, air filters, props, spark plugs, tapered wooden plugs to fit the sea cocks, water-pump impellers, and towing line.

- Teak trim is a mark of quality. Unfortunately, it's also a sign that the captain and crew spend a lot of time sanding and polishing. The best way to keep teak shipshape is to wash it down with a mild cleaner once a week. Every couple of weeks, after a thorough washing, oil should be applied. Varnish, for those who want a high-gloss finish, should be applied at the beginning, middle, and end of the season. The first step is to sand until the surfaces are uniformly dull, then dust and wipe with a rag. Finally, apply the varnish. Because fishermen would rather fish than polish teak, many boat builders are reducing teak trim or eliminating it completely.

- Tools are an important addition to every boat. A typical tool kit includes: duct tape, electrical tape, rope, wire, screwdriver set, ratchet set, wrench set, adjustable wrenches, channel locks, pliers, a strap wrench (for oil filters), prop wrench, vise grips, flashlights, soldering iron, solder, hammer, funnel, hacksaw, and knife.

- Zinc anodes are small pieces of metal that attach to rudders, shafts, and outdrives to protect them against electrolysis, a corrosive chemical reaction that happens to metals in the presence of an electric current. Electric current on boats can either be caused by ungrounded leakage from onboard 12-volt batteries or from a 120-volt shorepower circuit that has poor integrity. Electrolysis can also be caused by simply submerging the boat's collection of dissimilar metals in a warm-water bath. This is the basic composition of a battery. Since base metals (those that are low on the Periodic Table of Elements) corrode before noble metals (those that are high on the Periodic Table of Elements) when the two are in contact, zinc (the least noble metal available to fishermen) is used as a sacrificial anode. All zincs should be checked frequently and replaced when more than half is gone. This includes the zinc pencils located on inboard engines.

CHAPTER 8

SALTWATER GAMEFISH IDENTIFIER

Did you ever notice that the moment a fish strikes, top guides and fishermen know exactly what kind of fish it is? Somehow, they can name the fish even if it hits a bait fifty yards back, the seas are churning, and the beast immediately dives beneath the surface. Actually, that's not quite true. Elite fishermen like this know what kind of fish it is before it strikes the bait. How do they know? First of all, they have good eyes, and know where and when to look. More important, they know what they're seeing. Years of experience teaches them to seek out clues that are as revealing of identity as fingerprints—shape, color, marks, patterns, and fin configurations.

The following information will come in handy when it's time to identify a fish on the end of your line. The first step is to forget all about the scientific classification method, which is a large and confusing subject (actually, I don't wish to dismiss this important field completely, but it's too complex to delve into here). This body of knowledge is more for zool-

ogists than fishermen, with its numerous divisions—class, order, family, subfamily, tribe, genus, and species. Anglers simply want to know a fish's name, not its place in the overall scheme of nature.

Unfortunately, common names aren't necessarily common. One man's dolphin is another man's dorado or another man's mahimahi. To help clear up the confusion (or, more accurately, to maintain it at its current level), common names for each fish will be provided in this chapter, as well as popular alternatives where appropriate. In addition, the Latin names of fish will also be listed. Latin names are a well-established method of identification that's used by the scientific community throughout the world. By convention, the first letter of the first word in the Latin name (the genus) is always capitalized, but the second name (the species) is not. Knowing Latin names will help those anglers who wish to pursue further research.

In all instances, the scientific information presented in this chapter is derived from *Common and Scientific Names of Fishes from the United States and Canada,* Fifth Edition (1991, American Fisheries Society Special Publication #20), and *World Fishes Important to North Americans* (1991, American Fisheries Society Special Publication #21). To obtain copies of these publications, write to the American Fisheries Society, 5410 Maryland, Grosvenor Lane, Bethesda, MD 20814. Also helpful was *World Record Game Fishes* (1994 edition, published by the International Game Fish Association, 1301 E. Atlantic Boulevard, Pompano Beach, FL 33060).

Of the major physical clues used to identify fish, the most important is the shape or form. Few fishermen would mistake the flattened body of a flounder for the long, rounded bodies of barracuda. Coloration is the next-easiest clue, but this is frequently tricky. Shades of color are extremely variable from fish to fish, even within the same species. In addition, most fish possess the ability to change color under certain circumstances. To pin down identification, fishermen look for additional clues, such as patterns and markings. These key indicators include stripes, bars, spots, mottling, and so forth.

When a fish is finally brought to boat, anglers can then inspect a number of other key features. Chief among these are the fins (which includes the tail or caudal fin). The tail should be inspected for length, width, color, and markings. Fins should be inspected for placement and configuration. Finally, an inspection of the exterior body will reveal other important clues, including the type of scales, head, mouth, teeth, and gill plate.

One final note: While many fish discussed here are found in numerous corners of the globe, only U.S. ranges are given in this chapter.

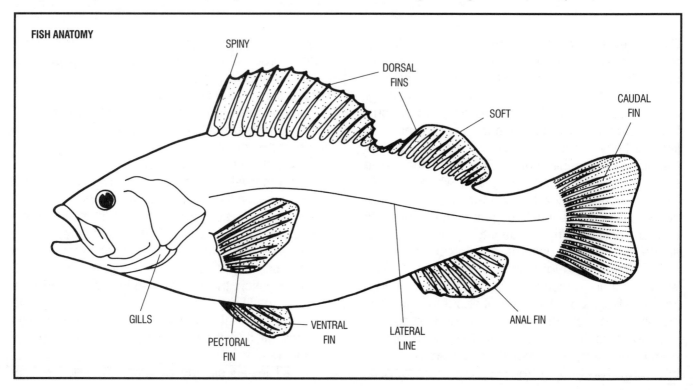

FISH ANATOMY

SPINY
DORSAL FINS
SOFT
CAUDAL FIN
GILLS
PECTORAL FIN
VENTRAL FIN
LATERAL LINE
ANAL FIN

BILLFISH

Characterized by long bills, majestic appearance, spectacular leaping ability, and an awesome fighting spirit, billfish are considered the catch of a lifetime. As with many other gamefish described in this section, billfish are threatened by commercial-fishing and environmental pressures, and so are strictly regulated. Fishermen should become familiar with catch limits and minimum sizes for retention. An increasing number of fishermen take great pains to make sure fish are released alive and fully recovered after the fight is over. In addition, many participate in scientific tagging programs. Both practices are highly recommended.

Blue marlin (*Makaira nigricans*) are magnificent offshore pelagic (wandering and migratory) fish found in both the Atlantic and Pacific oceans. Although black marlin catches have been larger than blues, there is evidence provided by longliners that blues may be the bigger fish. They average from two

hundred pounds to five hundred pounds, and probably top out in the neighborhood of two thousand pounds. In the eastern United States, they range from Florida to Cape Cod and throughout the Gulf of Mexico; on the West Coast, they're found mainly off Baja California and Hawaii. They are surface feeders that are typically caught by trolling natural or artificial bait. Chief characteristics include a high, anteriorly pointed dorsal fin and a cobalt-blue back with silvery white flanks and belly. Like all marlin, the flesh is good-tasting and sought after by most markets throughout the world, except in the United States, where sale of Atlantic marlin is prohibited in an effort to preserve the threatened species.

Black marlin (*Makaira indica*) are the other giants of the marlin family. Since they are only found on the West Coast off Baja California, or off Hawaii, they are a rare catch prized by most fishermen. Their size and feeding habits are similar to that of blue marlin. They are also similar in appearance, except that the blue's pectoral fins fold back against its body while

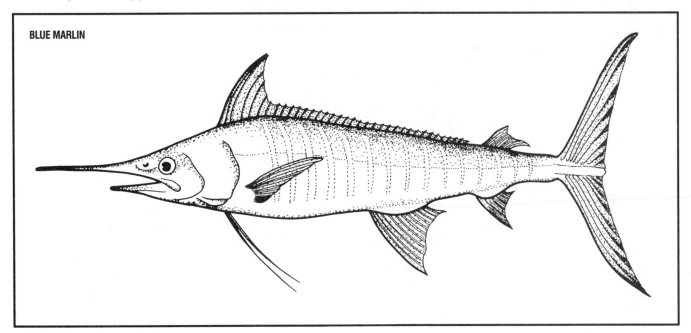

BLUE MARLIN

the black's pectoral fins are rigid and cannot be folded back.

White marlin (*Tetrapturus albidus*) are the smallest of the marlin and weigh from forty pounds to sixty pounds on average, although they can reach two hundred pounds. Their range is widespread, but limited to the East Coast from Florida to Cape Cod and throughout the Gulf of Mexico. Like blacks and blues, they are surface feeders that are typically caught by trolling. Whites are distinguished by a rounded tip on the first dorsal fin as well as rounded pectoral and anal fins. Their color is generally much lighter than other marlin. Often there are light-blue vertical bars on the flanks.

Striped marlin (*Tetrapturus audax*) are scattered widely throughout Pacific waters and are the most common marlin on the West Coast. Their range is normally restricted to Southern California and Hawaii, but occasionally they are found farther north. Average size is one hundred to two hundred pounds, and the upper limit is about five hundred pounds. Although trolling is the best method for catching striped marlin, their feeding habits are a lit-

tle different from other marlin. They are often spotted tailing or feeding on the surface, and sometimes can be caught by presenting them with bait. Striped marlin are characterized by an exceptionally high, pointed dorsal fin and flanks that have prominent bluish vertical stripes. The fins have iridescent blue spots and often turn neon blue.

Sailfish (*Istiophorus platyterus*) are by far the most abundant billfish found both on the East Coast, from Florida to Virginia and throughout the Gulf of Mexico, and on the West Coast, off Baja California. Although there's some apparent disparity in size between Atlantic and Pacific sails, they are actually the same species. Average size in the Atlantic is thirty to fifty pounds with a maximum of over one hundred pounds. Average size in the Pacific is between ninety and one hundred twenty-five pounds with a maximum of about two hundred pounds. Like marlin, sails are mostly surface feeders that are caught while trolling natural or artificial bait. In general, they are found fairly close to shore. Since their flesh is of poor quality, sails are invariably returned to the water. A huge, sail-like dorsal fin provides in-

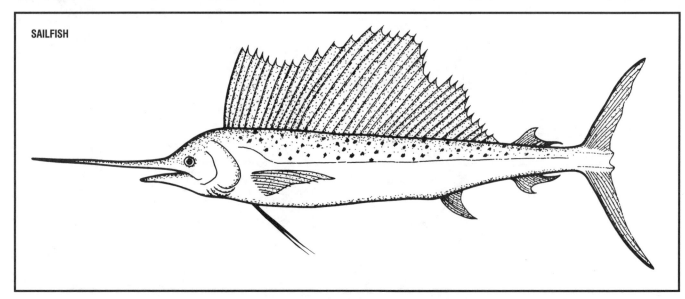

SAILFISH

stant identification. The body is generally bluish and scattered with black spots.

Two other billfish are rarely caught by sport fishermen: They are swordfish (*Xiphias gladius*) and spearfish, both longbill and shortbill. Like whales of old, sweet-tasting swordfish, or broadbills, are hunted worldwide in far offshore waters by fleets of commercial fishing boats. As a result, swordfish have virtually collapsed as a gamefish. Their range is from Cape Cod to Florida on the East Coast, and Southern California and Hawaii in the Pacific. Average size for swords diminishes each year and is now between one hundred and three hundred pounds, although a fully grown fish may nearly reach two thousand pounds. They feed deep at night and on the surface during the day, where they actually doze. Long lining, harpooning, and casting to surface fish are the most common fishing methods. Swords are characterized by long, flat bills and the lack of pelvic fins. The dorsal fin is high and sickle-shaped.

Spearfish are the least numerous of billfish and are found in far offshore waters. The longbill spear-

fish (*Tetrapturus pfluegeri*) is found in East Coast waters from Cape Cod to Florida and throughout the Gulf of Mexico. The shortbill spearfish (*Tetrapturus angustirostris*) is a Pacific species sometimes found off Hawaii. Spearfish are the smallest billfish and have slender bodies. They are characterized by a short bill that's not much longer than the lower jaw, and a vent forward of the anal fin. Average size is between thirty and forty pounds, with a maximum of about one hundred pounds. Most anglers catch spearfish while trolling or long lining for other species.

TUNA

While tuna don't make spectacular leaps and aren't equipped with the magnificent bills and dorsal fins of billfish, they are equally large trophy fish that put up ferocious fights. Like swordfish, tuna (especially bluefin) is a highly prized food fish that is subject to intense pressure by worldwide commercial fishing fleets. Consequently, their numbers have dropped

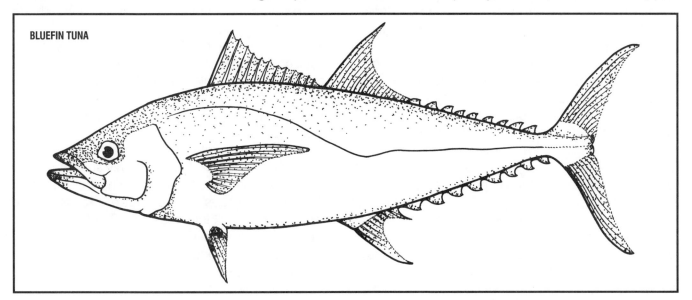

BLUEFIN TUNA

drastically in easily accessible coastal waters frequented by most sportfishermen. While daily limits and size restrictions are strictly regulated, few fishermen tag and release tuna. Bluefin tuna (headed and gutted) can bring of twenty dollars a pound, which is a fortune for catches that frequently weigh several hundred pounds.

Bluefin tuna (*Thunnus thynnus*) are the giants of the tuna family and often called the ocean's greatest fighting fish. Bringing one of these giants (between three hundred and two thousand pounds in the Atlantic) to boat can involve hours of hard work. The same is true for more typical catches, which average from over one hundred to three hundred pounds. When bluefin are found in schools, the average size runs from ten pounds to more than one hundred pounds. In the Atlantic, bluefin range from the Gulf of Mexico in the south to well north of Maine. In the Pacific, they are found in Southern California and Hawaii, and grow to about five hundred pounds. They are frequently found in nearshore waters. Chunking, slow trolling, and fishing with live bait are the preferred methods for catching these highly prized fish. They can be identified by short pectoral fins, high gill raker counts, and a striated liver.

Yellowfin tuna (*Thunnus albacares*), another prized food fish, has a somewhat different range from bluefin, although they are often caught in the same locations and are sometimes difficult to distinguish from their giant cousins. Typical range is from Florida to Cape Cod and throughout the Gulf of Mexico on the East Coast. In the Pacific, they can be found off Southern California and Hawaii. Average size runs between fifty and one hundred pounds, with a maximum of four hundred pounds. When first caught, yellowfins have golden upper sides and yellow fins. In some fish the second dorsal and anal fins are highly extended, but this isn't a uniform trait. Its surest identifying feature is a smooth liver. Feeding

habits and fishing methods are similar to bluefins with one exception—occasionally large yellowfin will hit a fast-trolled billfish lure.

Bigeye tuna (*Thunnus obesus*) are found in deep, far-offshore waters. Their range is from North Carolina to Cape Cod in the Atlantic and the entire West Coast in the Pacific, along with Hawaii. Despite this large range, their numbers are no longer abundant. Atlantic fish average between one hundred and two hundred pounds and go up to four hundred pounds. Pacific fish are probably the same size, but their average is down to about fifty to one hundred pounds due to commercial-fishing pressure. The fish are characterized by big eyes, long pectoral fins, and striated livers. Chunking at night is the surest method for catching bigeyes, although they sometimes hit live bait that's slow trolled during the day.

Albacore (*Thunnus alalunga*) is sometimes called a longfin, which is an apt name because its pectoral fins are greatly extended compared with other tuna. In addition, it has a relatively pale color and a slim body. Albacore (known as white-meat tuna in the can) is an abundant species that has a worldwide range. It can be found along the entire lengths of both coasts, including southern Alaska in the Pacific. Average size is between twenty and fifty pounds (a bit smaller in the Pacific), with an upper limit of about ninety pounds. Slow trolling with live bait and chunking are the preferred fishing methods.

There are several other tuna that deserve mention, although they are not as highly sought as their previously mentioned cousins. The blackfin tuna (*Thunnus atlanticus*) is the smallest Atlantic tuna, and is found from Florida to North Carolina. Average catches run from five to twenty-five pounds, and peak at about fifty pounds. These schooling fish can be identified by uniformly dark finlets that lack the typical yellow coloration. Skipjack tuna (*Katsu-*

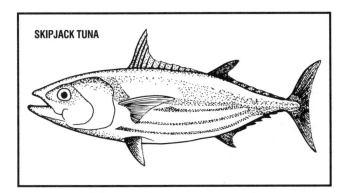

SKIPJACK TUNA

wonus pelamis) are recognized by distinctive horizontal stripes on the belly and sides. They range in schools in both the Atlantic, from Florida to Cape Cod, and Pacific, along the entire coast. Skipjacks are also called striped tuna and watermelon tuna. Since their meat is relatively dark and soft, it is not highly prized, although it is used for low-priced canned tuna. Average size runs from three to twelve pounds, with an upper limit of about forty pounds. Little tunny (*Euthynnus alletteratus*) is identified by a scattering of spots below the pectoral fins and wavy stripes on the back. Other names for these fierce-fighting fish are false albacore, and little tuna. They are nearshore feeders that can be caught by artificial lures, either cast or trolled. Since their flesh is of poor quality, most fishermen either release them or use them for bait. Little tunny are typically in the five- to fifteen-pound range, although they can grow to more than thirty-five pounds.

MACKEREL

All mackerel are good eating fish and fine fighters that challenge a light-tackle angler's skill. These slim, streamlined pelagic Atlantic Ocean fish are often found migrating in large schools, except for wahoo, which are solitary wanderers found world-wide in warmer waters.

Wahoo (*Acanthocybium solandri*) are the most highly prized of the mackerel family and one of off-shore fishing's most spectacular jumpers and fighters. They are noted for leaping strikes and blistering initial runs, hence the myth that the name derives from an angler's typical reaction. Closer to the truth: In the Pacific Ocean the fish is called oahu, also Pacific Kingfish. Wahoo are easy to identify with long, slender bodies, small mouths filled with sharp teeth, and vertical bars on the flanks. As noted, their range is worldwide in warmer offshore waters, especially in the Gulf of Mexico, and from Florida to Cape Cod in the Atlantic and off Baja California and Hawaii in the Pacific. Average catches are between twenty and sixty pounds; however, they can grow to one hundred fifty pounds. They are surface and middle-depth feeding fish that are renowned as one of the finest eating fish in the world. They are caught by trolling.

King mackerel (*Scomberomorus cavalla*) are a popular commercial and sportfish that range from Texas to Virginia. Often called kingfish or giant

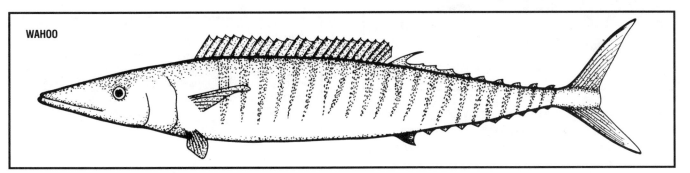

WAHOO

mackerel, king mackerel favor reefs and a variety of inshore habitat. Average size runs between five and thirty pounds, and tops out at more than one hundred pounds. Kings have a silvery green tint and are absent of the typical mackerel's distinctive yellow body spots. They are, in fact, the least colorful of the mackerel family. Commercial netting caused a collapse in the mackerel fishery a few years ago and the species has come under strict regulation. Trolling and live baiting are effective fishing techniques.

Spanish mackerel (*Scomberomorus maculatus*) are the smallest and most abundant of sportfish mackerel. Like kingfish, they are found in inshore waters; however, their range is somewhat larger, extending from Florida to Cape Cod and throughout the Gulf of Mexico. The Spanish are distinguished by the round yellow spots that appear on their silvery flanks. Average sizes are from one to five pounds, although they can grow to twenty pounds.

Cero mackerel (*Scomberomorus regalis*) is the least-common mackerel and is rarely found in schools. It is larger than the Spanish and has a limited range. Few are caught outside of southern Florida; however, they have been known to venture throughout the Gulf of Mexico and north to the mid-

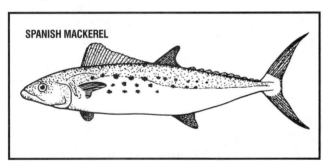

SPANISH MACKEREL

Atlantic. Ceros typically range between five and fifteen pounds, and occasionally run to thirty-five pounds. Like the Spanish, ceros have yellow spots; however, they are somewhat elongated and ar-

ranged in rows. They also have a yellow line running along the midsection.

DRUM

This large family of fish gets its name from an ability to produce sound by vibrating muscles near the swim bladder, which acts as an amplification box. There are about two hundred members of this family and almost all favor shallow, inshore waters.

Red drum (*Sciaenops ocellatus*) is a member of the drum family that few will mistake for any of the other cousins. Its unique copper color and back spot at the base of the tail make it quite distinctive. Most anglers know the species as redfish or occasionally channel bass, and look for them on sandbars, marsh banks, and tidal flats. They are fine eating fish. Today, their retention is stricly regulated and they are making a comeback from a near-total collapse. The average size catch for redfish is between five and twenty pounds, with trophies running nearly to one hundred pounds. Their range extends from Texas to Virginia. Retention of red drum is strictly regulated due to over harvest.

Black drum (*Pogonias cromis*) are similar to redfish in size, range, and taste; however, they are much less prized by anglers. Two primary reasons are that they don't put up the same spectac-

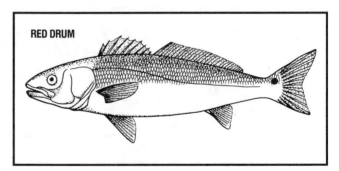

RED DRUM

ular fight and they are suprisingly difficult to clean because of extremely heavy scales. Black drum are stockier than redfish and have no spot on the tail.

Spotted sea trout (*Cynoscion nebulosus*) and weakfish (*Cynoscion regalis*) are similar in appearance and size; however, the spotted trout is differentiated by numerous round black spots on the flanks, dorsal fin, and tail. It is also slightly smaller. Average catches are in the two- to six-pound range, but the fish can reach twenty pounds. Their ranges overlap in the South and Mid-Atlantic states; however, the spotted sea trout is rarely found north of Virginia. Both frequent shallow waters. The name weakfish is commonly applied to fish of the genus *Cynoscion,* and refers to the tender mouth membrane that is easily torn and enables the fish to escape from the hook.

White sea bass (*Atractoscion nobilis*) are the chief West Coast representative of the drum family, and they are found as far north as San Francisco. Similar in appearance to a weakfish or a spotted sea trout, white sea bass have a raised ridge along the midline of the belly and look like nothing else their size in the Pacific. The fish are usually found around kelp beds and are good eating. Average size is in the seven- to fifteen-pound range. The upper limit is about eighty pounds.

SEA BASS

This large, bottom-dwelling family may not be composed of flashy fighters, but pulling the largest specimens from the bottom can be a good challenge. Brought to shore, all of them are good to eat. Most prefer inshore waters.

Black sea bass (*Centropristes striatus*) are the only cool-water member of the sea bass family, and their range is the inshore waters from northern

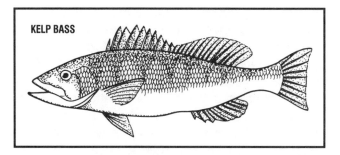

Florida to Cape Cod. Average size is from one to three pounds, with an upper limit of ten pounds. They're characterized by stocky bodies, a dark hump on top of the head, and an elongated upper lobe on the tail.

Kelp bass (*Paralabrax clathratus*) live up to their name and are typically found around kelp beds on the West Coast as far north as the Santa Barbara area. Although average catches are in the one- to two-pound range, they can reach fifteen pounds. Their coloration is brown to olive green with light blotches. They are also called calico bass.

Giant Sea Bass (*Stereolepis gigas*) are true giants of the West Coast that range as far north as the Santa Barbara area. Although they can grow to nearly six hundred pounds, the typical catch is in the neighborhood of fifty to one hundred pounds. This rare fish has suffered severe depletion and there is a current moratorium on their retention. The fish are characterized by large mouths, dark brown bodies, and spots on the sides.

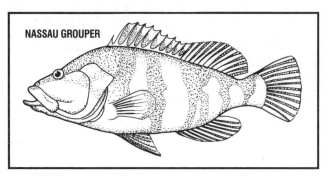

Nassau grouper (*Epinephelus striatus*) are a common member of the grouper family, with a range that runs throughout the Gulf of Mexico and in the Atlantic as far north as the Carolinas. Their fine-tasting meat is much prized by fishermen. Distinctive characteristics include a dark blotch in the saddle at the base of the tail and dark vertical bars on the head and body. Average size is from three to ten pounds, with large Nassaus coming in at fifty-five pounds.

Other members of the grouper family are: jewfish (*Epinephelus itajara*), which tip the scales at as much as eight hundred pounds and are limited in range to Florida in the Atlantic and throughout the Gulf of Mexico; yellowfin grouper (*Mycteroperca nenenosa*), which are typically found in the same range and top out at about thirty-five pounds; red grouper (*Epinephelus morio*), which range throughout the Gulf of Mexico and north to the Carolinas and weigh up to thirty pounds; gag grouper (*Mycteroperca microlepis*), which have a similar range and weigh up to sixty pounds; and black grouper (*Mycteroperca bonaci*), which are limited to Florida and can weigh up to one hundred pounds.

COD

Although considered to be commercial food fish, the bottom-dwelling cod family is readily accessible to anglers in the Northeast. While not a gamefish, several of these cool-water species are of special interest to both inshore and offshore sportfishermen. They are noted for their elongated bodies and spineless fins.

Atlantic cod (*Gadus morhua*) are a prime target for commercial fishing fleets and can be caught by anglers around offshore humps and wrecks from Virginia to Maine. They are distinguished by three dorsal fins and two anal fins. Modern cod top out at about one hundred pounds; they average from five pounds to thirty pounds. Although prolific, they are threatened by commercial-fishing pressure, and their retention is regulated.

Pollock (*Pollachius virens*) are a more active predator than cod and more aggressive fighters; however, their flesh is less tasty and they are less prized. Their range is from New Jersey to Maine. Average catches are in the five- to thirty-pound neighborhood, with the top limit about sixty pounds.

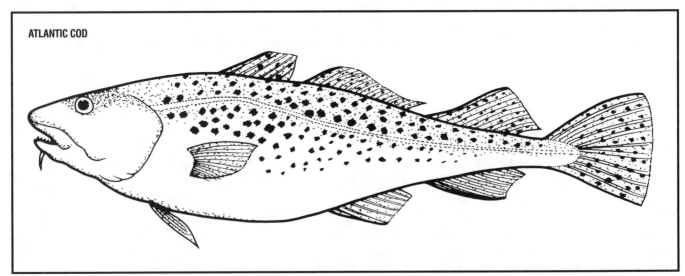

ATLANTIC COD

Pollock are characterized by a forked tail and a prominent pale line running horizontally across dark flanks.

Haddock (*Melanogrammus aeglefinus*) are similar in appearance and range to the pollock. They are distinguished by a black patch just above the pectoral fin and a black horizontal line running across the flanks. They are also more typically found offshore than pollock, which can be caught inshore. They are highly regarded as a food fish and average catches are from three pounds to six pounds. At the upper end they can grow to about thirty-five pounds.

The hake family is closely related to the cod family and occupies similar cold-water territory, from Virginia to Maine. They can be caught in inshore waters and around deep-water wrecks. The family includes: red hake (*Urophycis chuss*), which is a small, red-bodied fish (smaller than eight pounds) that can be good to eat if properly handled (sometimes called ling); silver hake (*Merluccius bilinearis*), which have silvery sides and a toothy mouth, are small food fish that typically average much less than their eight-pound upper limit (also called whitefish); and white hake (*Urophycis tenuis*), which look like giant red hake with a purple sheen, are the giants of the family, growing to sixty pounds.

FLOUNDER

One of the most peculiar, looking fish in the ocean, flounder are bottom-dwelling fish that have flat, frying-pan bodies and the unique ability to migrate one eye from the bottom to the top of the head. All are superb to eat, and like the cod family are considered food fish.

Summer flounder (*Paralichthys dentatus*) are Atlantic Ocean fish that range from the Carolinas to Cape Cod. This popular, inshore food fish is sometimes called fluke, and grows to about twenty-five pounds, although catches of one to four pounds are more typical. It has a brown coloration, a toothy mouth, and spots on the top part of the body. Overfishing has depleted summer flounder and forced strict retention regulations.

Winter flounder (*Pseudopleuronectes americanus*) is a northerly, inshore cousin to the summer flounder, with a range that goes from Delaware to Maine. A small fish, averaging about a pound (and topping out at ten pounds), it has a rust-colored body and a tiny mouth.

California halibut (*Paralichthys californicus*) are inshore Pacific flounder that are distinguished by large, toothy mouths and a dark horizontal line across the flanks that arches high over the pectoral fin. Although typical catches are small, in the two- to ten-pound range, they can reach seventy pounds. They are commonly found as far north as San Francisco.

Pacific halibut (*Hippoglossus stenolepis*) have a wide range that extends from the Santa Barbara area north to Alaska and the Bering Sea. While these giants average from ten to one hundred pounds, they are known to grow to more than five hundred pounds. As a highly valuable food fish, Pacific halibut are strictly regulated.

JACKS

Jacks are typically large, fast fish that are possessed with a never-say-die fighting spirit. The reason the family isn't highly regarded by fishermen is that the meat is generally dark, unappetizing, and susceptible to carrying the debilitating human disease known as ciguatera poisoning. With about one hundred forty members in the family, there are few universal characteristics. Most typical are prominently forked tails and narrow caudal peduncles.

Greater amberjack (*Seriola dumerili*) are the

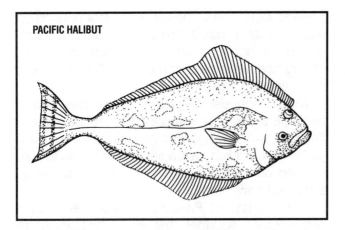

PACIFIC HALIBUT

largest of the jack family and are easily identified by a black stripe that runs along light flanks from the tail to the eye. They are relatively streamlined as far as jacks go. Their range is from Florida north to Virginia and throughout the Gulf of Mexico. Sizes average thirty pounds to fifty pounds and top out at more than one hundred seventy pounds. They feed along deep-water wrecks, reefs, humps, oil rigs, and buoys. They are rarely eaten unless smoked.

Jack crevalle (*Caranx hippos*) are found in a variety of inshore waters from Florida to Cape Cod and throughout the Gulf. A dark spot on the pectoral fin and gill cover helps distinguish the jack crevalle from other jacks. Other characteristics are a broad body and a blunt forehead. Average sizes

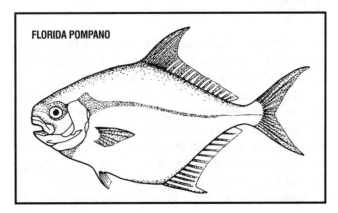

FLORIDA POMPANO

run from three to fifteen pounds. Large ones top out at fifty pounds. Like amberjack, these fish are rarely eaten.

Florida pompano (*Trachinotus carolinus*) are highly prized as the best-tasting fish in the jack family, but they are rarely caught from boats. Most are caught by surfcasting from the shore. Their shallow-water territory runs from Florida to North Carolina and throughout the Gulf of Mexico. The fish average about two pounds, but they can tip the scales at more than eight pounds. They are characterized by a round profile and a silvery golden hue.

African pompano (*Alectis ciliaris*) are bigger than their Florida cousins but less prized by anglers. They also have a more limited range, extending no farther north than Florida in the Atlantic and sometimes as far north as the Louisiana oil rigs in the Gulf of Mexico. Silver coloring, wide body, and steep forehead are the African's chief physical characteristics. These inshore fish are typically found near reefs and wrecks. Average-size catches are from ten to thirty pounds; adults occasionally reach fifty pounds. Like the jack crevalle and amberjack, Africans are seldom kept by fishermen for their dinner tables.

Permit (*Trachinotus falcatus*) are considered one of the world's great fighting fish, but unfortunately, their nearest range extends no farther than Southern Florida. Typically found on shallow reefs and tidal flats, and occasionally in schools over wrecks, permit are best caught with live bait off light tackle. Average size is five to twenty-five pounds, although they can grow to as much as sixty pounds. The meat is not prized and most fishermen release them.

Yellowtail (*Seriola lalandi dorsalis*), which like sea trout could be considered misnamed, are found on the West Coast north to about Santa Barbara. Average catches run from seven to fifteen pounds, and have been known to grow to more than eighty

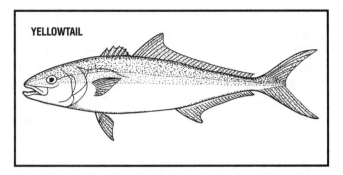

YELLOWTAIL

pounds. Coloration on this distinctive fish is blue-green on the back and upper flanks and silver below. A light yellow stripe runs horizontally down the middle of the flank from the snout to the tail, which is also yellow. Unlike most other jacks, yellowtail are highly sought after (around kelp beds) as both food and gamefish.

SHARKS

Although widely renowned as the fiercest predators in the ocean and the most dangerous to humans, sharks are actually a huge family of fish that includes everything from tiny aquarium-size fish to docile plankton eaters. The sharks covered here are the species most commonly sought or caught. They are distinguished by five to seven pairs of gill openings, skin with a sandpaper texture, a body shaped like a torpedo, and prominent teeth.

Shortfin mako sharks (*Isurus oxyrhynchus*) are noted for their spectacular leaps and sweet-tasting meat. They are the most highly prized gamefish in the shark family. Identification characteristics include a cobalt-blue color on the back and long, slender, curved teeth that protrude from the mouth. They also have a streamlined shape, a nearly symmetrical crescent-shaped tail, and a pointed snout. Their range in the East is throughout the Gulf of Mexico and along the entire Atlantic Coast. In the Pacific they are found off California, where they are sometimes called bonito shark, and off Hawaii. Average size is about fifty pounds to two hundred pounds, although they can grow to more than eleven hundred pounds. Smaller sizes are typical in the Pacific. As in fishing all sharks, chumming well offshore is the pre-

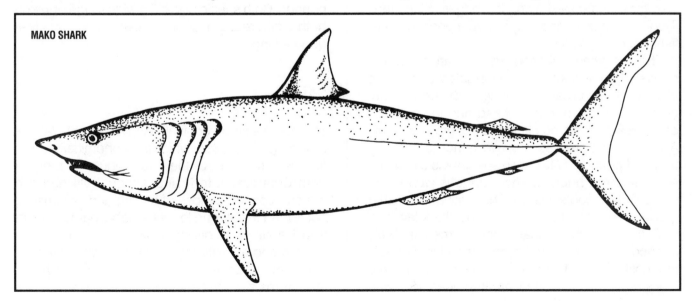

MAKO SHARK

ferred method. They have been known to attack humans, bite boats, and leap into cockpits.

White sharks (*Carcharodon carcharias*), often called great white sharks, are not the largest fish in the shark family, but they are known to grow to two tons, and possibly larger. Their range is worldwide, but they are primarily found in cooler seas, and often inshore. Few fishermen actually fish for whites because they are relatively rare. Their fame is primarily due to attacks on humans, which are even more rare. The white has a grayish-brown back that fades to off-white on the belly and black-tipped pectoral fins. Another distinctive feature are large, triangular teeth with serrated edges.

Blue sharks (*Prionace glauca*) have a similar range to the whites, but they stay farther offshore and are much more abundant. Average catches run between fifty and two hundred pounds, with Pacific fish averaging a bit smaller. Record catches are in the neighborhood of four hundred pounds. The blue has a long, slender body with a pointed snout and long, sickle-shaped pectoral fins. The back is light blue and the belly is white. The teeth are mostly triangular and serrated along the edges. Since their flesh is not prized, and they put up a poor fight, few fishermen target blues.

Thresher sharks (*Alopias vulpinus*) are easily recognized by the enormously elongated upper lobe of their tail, which can be as long as the body. Other characteristics are a small head and teeth, and a dark back that can be either brown, gray, or black. Average sizes are between two hundred and four hundred pounds; fully grown specimens can reach eight hundred pounds. Their range is worldwide, particularly in cooler waters. The meat of a thresher is considered among the best in the shark family.

Of the other sharks that sportfishermen are likely to encounter, the spirited hammerhead is probably the most familiar. The great hammerhead (*Sphyrna mokarran*), the scalloped hammerhead (*Sphyrna lewini*), and the smooth hammerhead (*Sphyrna zygaena*) are the three most common species. The great hammerhead is the largest of the clan and grows to about one thousand pounds. In general, hammerheads prefer warmer, offshore waters. Because of the distinctive form of their T-shaped heads the hammerhead family is easily identified. Individual species within the family are somewhat difficult to distinguish.

Sandbar sharks (*Carcharhinus milberti*) and dusky sharks (*Carcharhinus obscurus*) are similar in appearance and range. Both are round-nosed, gray-brown in color, and have a distinctive ridge between the dorsal fins. Many anglers know sandbar sharks as brown sharks. They distinguish between duskys and browns by noting the brown's higher dorsal fin and placement farther forward in relation to the pectoral fins. Of the two, the dusky is the larger, and can grow to more than six hundred pounds with an average catch being between one hundred and two hundred pounds. Sandbar or brown sharks are about half that size, with an average catch being between thirty and one hundred pounds. Both species inhabit a wide range of waters both offshore and inshore. Browns make relatively good eating.

SALMON

The name salmon originally applied to only Atlantic salmon (*Salmo solar*), which is taxonomically classified as a member of the trout genus. Its range is from Connecticut to Maine, although its numbers are so depleted by loss of habitat and commercial net fishing that it is no longer a viable gamefish. The troutlike Atlantic is distinguished by a silvery color in the sea and a scattering of small black spots. In inland waters, especially at spawning time, the Atlantic turns a much darker bronze or brown.

Called an anadromous species, because it migrates from the sea to freshwater to spawn, salmon are often fished by using freshwater techniques outside the scope of this book. In the fisheries still available to saltwater fishermen, they typically use downriggers to fish a column of water well below the surface. The salmon's need to migrate to fresh water makes it an easy fish to net at river mouths, and consequently worldwide stocks of wild salmon are on the verge of total collapse. The sweet-tasting meat is still common table fare due to an abundance of fish farms.

Early North American settlers erroneously applied the name salmon to a completely different West Coast genus, *Oncorhynchus*. Although it has been proposed that the name Atlantic salmon be changed to end confusion concerning its relationship to trout, the name is deeply rooted in history and accepted worldwide.

The largest true salmon is the chinook salmon (*Oncorhynchus tshawtyscha*), or king salmon, which is found from Northern California to Alaska. Kings can grow to about one hundred twenty-five pounds and put up a fierce battle when hooked, two characteristics that make them highly prized by fishermen. One way to distinguish the spotted, silvery kings from other salmon is their black mouths and gums.

Coho salmon (*Oncorhynchus kisutch*) can be distinguished from kings by their paler mouths and

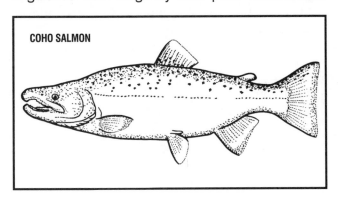

COHO SALMON

spotting that occurs only on the top portion of the tails. While the coho fishery has been mostly depleted in its original habitat, from Northern California to Alaska, extensive stocking efforts have kept the species available to sportfishermen in some transplanted locations, especially the Great Lakes. Cohos can reach weights of more than thirty pounds, although six- to twelve-pound catches are typical.

Sockeye salmon (*Oncorhynchus nerka*), although wonderful eating, are rarely caught by saltwater fishermen because they are plankton eaters. Their range is similar to that of the chinook or coho salmon, and they are distinguished by bright red bodies, especially when spawning. Fly-fishing techniques work best with sockeyes.

OTHER COMMON SPECIES

Some of the best fighting and eating fish don't fall into the above families. Many are either the sole member of their family of interest to anglers or, in some cases, the sole member of their family, period.

Atlantic bonito (*Sarda sarda*) are easily identified by characteristic black stripes that radiate along the back. They average between three to seven pounds, and some reach nearly twenty pounds. Their range is limited to the Atlantic Coast between Delaware and Cape Cod.

Bluefish (*Pomatomus salatrix*) rank as the most popular inshore gamefish in the Northeast from Delaware to Maine. They are also caught south to Florida and in the Gulf of Mexico, but in far fewer numbers. The most prominent feature on the relatively bland bluefish is its comparatively large mouth and sharp teeth, which can easily slice a careless fisherman's hand. Known as voracious eaters, schooling bluefish migrate between inshore and offshore waters. Their size averages from one to ten pounds, with an upper limit of more than thirty pounds. Daily catch limits have been placed on blues in recent years. As a food fish, their meat is good-tasting but oily and doesn't keep well.

Bonefish (*Albula vulpes*) get their name because their flesh is filled with bones, which makes them virtually inedible. However, the enjoyment is in the catching, and bonefish are considered one of saltwater's premiere light-tackle gamefish. Excellent eyesight and natural wariness make bonefish a challenge to stalk, and sizzling runs make them difficult to reel in. Found mainly inshore on South Florida's tidal flats, slender bones have silvery bodies, sloping foreheads, and longitudinal stripes on the back. They grow up to twenty pounds, but typical catches are between three and eight pounds.

California barracuda (*Sphyraena argentae*), unlike the great barracuda of the East Coast, are edible food fish that need not be thrown back. Their range extends as far north as the Santa Barbara area. Their size averages from two to five pounds, with an upper limit of about twenty pounds. Like all barracuda, they have elongated bodies with a toothy mouth.

California sheepshead (*Semicossyphus pulcher*) are West Coast fish that have distinctly different appearances between genders. The females are pinkish, and the males are black on the front and rear thirds of the body. Both have lumps on the head and a mouth with prominent teeth. As with many fish, they start out in life as females and become males later on. Their range extends north in California to about Monterey. Average catch is between two and five pounds, although the good-eating species can grow to forty pounds.

Canary rockfish (*Sebastes pinniger*) are bottom-feeding, West Coast fish that are caught in both inshore and offshore waters. An orange body and fins make them easy to identify. Although small (averag-

ing between one and two pounds), canary rockfish are sought after for their sweet-tasting meat. They can grow to about twelve pounds. Their range is from Southern California to Washington.

Cobia (*Rachycentron canadum*) are a large, fine-eating fish that put up a good fight right to the moment they're thrown into the fish box. This makes them a fisherman's favorite. Average sizes run from ten to fifty pounds. On the upper end, they can hit about one hundred fifty pounds. Their chief characteristics are a flat head and a brown upper body. They also have a dark-brown stripe that runs from the snout to the tail. Their range extends from Virginia south through the Gulf of Mexico, where they are sometimes called ling and lemonfish. They're often found around wrecks, floating objects, buoys, and oil rigs.

Dolphin (*Coryphaena hippurus*), as all fishermen know, are not what landlubbers refer to as "Flipper." Perhaps better names are the common alternatives of mahimahi or dorado. While the bodies of dolphins can be either bright yellow, green, or blue, few fishermen mistake their unique appearance: high forehead, lack of snout, and tall dorsal fin that extends nearly the full length of the body. Dolphin are among the most numerous of the offshore, surface-feeding gamefish and are found in warm waters worldwide. In the United States, they are found throughout the Gulf of Mexico, from Florida to Cape Cod in the Atlantic, and off Hawaii in the Pacific (only rarely in

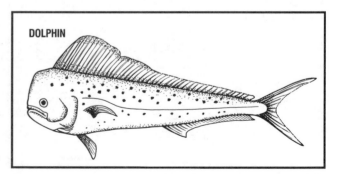
DOLPHIN

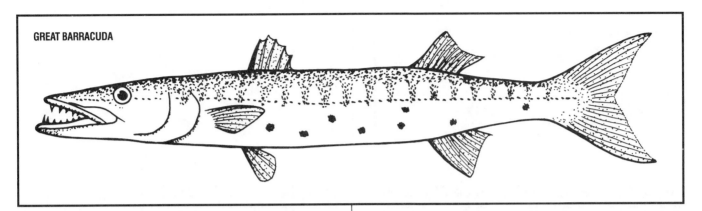

GREAT BARRACUDA

Southern California). Dolphin have light-colored meat that is considered a delicacy. Average catches are from five to fifteen pounds. On the upper end, they can reach ninety pounds. Dolphin are outstanding leapers when hooked.

Great barracuda (*Sphyraena barracuda*), with their large, toothy mouths and elongated, silvery bodies (with regularly spaced black blotches), are fine fighters but not recommended for eating. The reason to stay away from barracuda is that they are sometimes carriers of a debilitating human disease called ciguatera, which is common in many mature, predatory reef fish. Their size averages from three to fifteen pounds, but fully grown, they can reach ninety pounds. They are found throughout the Gulf of Mexico and north in the Atlantic to the Carolinas.

Lingcod (*Ophiodon clongatus*) has become increasingly popular with West Coast bottom fishermen in recent years. The species is characterized by a large, toothy mouth, dark blotches on the long body, and a long dorsal fin. Their range is in the cooler waters north of central California all the way to Alaska. Average catches for this good-eating fish are from five to twenty pounds.

Red snapper (*Lutjanus campechanus*) is an offshore bottom dweller with a stocky, red body and red fins and eyes. Its range in the Atlantic is from Florida to the Carolinas, and throughout the Gulf of Mexico. Although a fine-tasting fish with important commercial value, they are sought out by few anglers for sport. Average size is between five and fifteen pounds, with an upper limit of about forty pounds.

Sheepshead (*Archosargus probatocephalus*) are large members of the porgy family and are impossible to confuse with any other fish. Alternating bands of black and silver prominently adorn their flanks. Their range along the Atlantic Coast once extended farther north, but today, it runs only from the Carolinas to Florida and throughout the Gulf of Mexico. Average sizes for this good-eating, inshore fish are from two to five pounds. The giants, however, can reach thirty pounds.

Snook (*Centropomus undecimalis*) are a warmwater fish found on inshore tidal flats and mangroves of Florida in the Atlantic and throughout the Gulf of Mexico. Slender snook are characterized by a prominent black horizontal line running across silver flanks. Typical catches are in the five- to fifteen-pound range, although the species can tip the scales at as much as fifty pounds. They are excellent eating.

Striped bass (*Morone saxatilis*) are one of the most important game and food fish of the Northeast (where it is called rockfish). Their range extends all

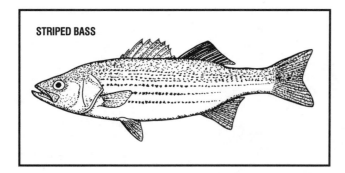

STRIPED BASS

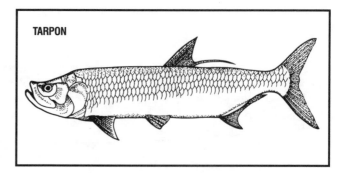

TARPON

the way from Georgia to Maine in the Atlantic and from San Francisco to Oregon in the Pacific. The West Coast fish were transplanted from Atlantic stocks in the late 1800s. This hardy fish is characterized by a white belly and a half dozen or more black stripes that run along silvery flanks. It inhabits a variety of inshore waters, including freshwater rivers. Average catches are on the modest side, running between three and fifteen pounds. However, the giants top out at more than eighty pounds.

Tarpon (*Megalops atlanticus*), also called silver king, are shallow-water giants considered to be one of the premiere challenges for light-tackle fishermen. Their leaping and fighting ability is legendary. They are distinguished by a large, under-slung mouth, silvery color, large scales, and a long filament on the back of the dorsal fin. With no taste incentive to

bring them to the dinner table, virtually all tarpon are released. Catches run the gamut from five to one hundred pounds; however, fully grown adults can tip the scales at more than two hundred pounds. Prime tarpon grounds are found on both coasts of Florida, but their territory extends throughout the Gulf of Mexico and north to the Carolinas.

Tautog (*Tautoga onitis*) are East Coast bottom dwellers that range from the Carolinas to Maine. In the New York City area, they are often referred to as blackfish. In the Chesapeake area, they are often called black porgy. This stout inshore fish is identified by a wide caudal peduncle, dark brown or black mottled flanks, and a long dorsal fin. It grows to about twenty-five pounds, but typical catches are from one to five pounds. Cleaned properly, they are a very good-eating fish.

GLOSSARY

Aft cabin—secondary sleeping quarters located beneath the helm, aft deck, or cockpit. It is typically characterized by a low ceiling, small hatches, and double berths. Sometimes called a mid cabin.

Backing down—shifting a powerboat into reverse during battle with a hooked fish.

Belly—occurs in a line when a fish makes a hard charge and changes direction before the line can be retrieved.

Belly rails—waist-high support rails on a spotting platform.

Biaxial fiberglass—a fiberglass reinforcement cloth that's made in a finely stitched basket-weave pattern.

Bilge—the lowest point of a boat's inner hull. It is typically drained by a bilge pump.

Bimini top—a simple protective canvas top mounted on tubular aluminum or stainless-steel supports. It is typically fixed to the gunwales and pulled taut by tie-down straps.

Catamaran—a twin-hulled boat that is exceptionally stable at rest in rolling seas and provides an exceptional rough-water ride.

Center-console boat—a type of boat with a planing V hull, foam flotation, and usually a gas engine, typically an outboard. It gets its name from the distinctive center-console component: a raised control unit mounted amidships. This unit can be either integrated into the mold of the deck or bolted on separately.

Chart plotter—an electronic navigation system that consists of a display screen and high-powered computer. It interfaces with such other helm instruments as radar, depth-finders, GPS, loran, and an auto pilot. It provides real-time course graphics, and can store and display hundreds of waypoints, chart marks, and routes. Some can interface with cartridge drives that display an electronic library of highly detailed maps.

Chart recorder—a depth-sounder that records data about bottom structure on paper.

111

Chine—the point on a hull where the sides and bottom intersect.

Chopped fiberglass—a mass of loose fiberglass fibers mixed with resin. It's sprayed into a mold by using a device called a chopper gun.

Chumming—a fishing technique done with finely chopped or ground particles of fish trailed in the water behind the boat. The goal is to use the scent of food to lure hungry gamefish toward the boat. Chunking is similar to chumming, except that chunks of bait are added to the ground-fish particles.

Coaming—refers to the interior cockpit portion of the gunwale. It is sometimes padded.

Companionway—an entryway to a belowdecks cabin.

Convertible—a type of a high-performance, extended-cruising, saltwater fishing boat typically equipped with a flying bridge, deckhouse, and belowdecks cabins. It is the largest and most luxurious boat in saltwater fishing.

Coring material—bulky, lightweight material placed between fiberglass laminates to provide strength and thickness, but little weight. Typical coring materials are polyurethane foam, balsa wood, and mat infused with micro balloons.

Counter rotation—refers to props spinning in opposite directions in twin-engine installations.

Cuddy cabin—a relatively small forward belowdecks area that typically includes a berth, marine head, and other amenities.

Cure—process in which the resins in a fiberglass-laminate compound harden through a chemical reaction caused by a catalyst.

Curtains—front and side enclosures that keep out wind, rain, and spray. These curtains are typically zippered into place and made of canvas and clear plastic.

Deadrise—the angle of V that each half of a hull makes in relation to the waterline. It is measured in degrees and sometimes called a dihedral.

Deep jigging—a fishing technique that allows anglers to fish a complete column of water from the bottom to the surface.

Deep-V hull—developed by Boston-based naval architect C. Raymond Hunt in the late 1950s, it is generally a knifelike, constant-V hull with a deadrise of 18° and higher.

Depth-sounder—also called a fish-finder. An electronic instrument that uses sonar to determine information about what's going on beneath the boat, including locating fish.

Diesel engine—an inboard, four-cycle internal-combustion engine that burns relatively small amounts of diesel fuel under great compression at low rpm.

Differential GPS (Global Positioning Satellite)—called DGPS, it is capable of producing position-fixing accuracy to within fifteen feet. In addition to receiving GPS satellite data, Differential Beacon Receivers (DBRs) also receive position-correction signals transmitted on a different frequency by land-based units. It is currently in the prototype stage.

Displacement—a measurement in pounds of the weight of water that a floating boat displaces.

Displacement hull—a bottom design that runs through the water (displacing it) rather than on top of the water. This type of design is characterized by slow, steady, efficient operation.

Downrigger—an electronic or manual rod-and-reel unit mounted to the gunwale and used for deep-water trolling. It sends a wire line weighted by a heavy ball or plane to a controlled depth. The ball or plane is fitted with a short wire and a clip that holds the fisherman's line and releases it when a fish strikes.

Double chine—a hull feature that occurs at the point where the bottom and the sides intersect, and where a hard chine combines with a reverse chine to form a complex geometric shape.

Dual-console boat—a hybrid fishing boat that

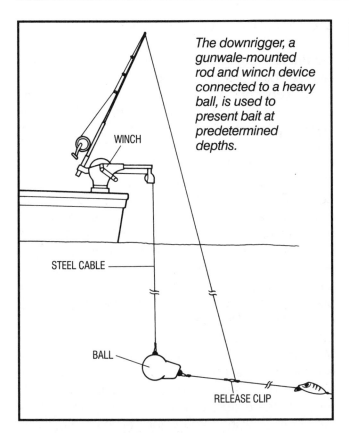

WINCH

STEEL CABLE

BALL

RELEASE CLIP

The downrigger, a gunwale-mounted rod and winch device connected to a heavy ball, is used to present bait at predetermined depths.

works well in both saltwater and freshwater environments. It is characterized by a split or walk-through console and typically has an open bow. Many fishermen use these boats for double duty—both fishing and entertaining. Similar in design to a freshwater bowrider runabout.

EPIRB—the acronym stands for *e*mergency *p*osition *i*ndicating *r*adio *b*eacon. When the unit is activated, it transmits an emergency radio signal to a network of satellites that identify the boat the EPIRB is on, and pinpoints its location.

Express boat—a hybrid fishing boat that's also known as an open boat, an open express, or an express fisherman. The basic design is composed of a wide-open cockpit that leads directly to a helm station located on the same level or raised up a step or

two. Cabins are located belowdecks.

Fiberglass—a nonhomogeneous composite plastic made from resins and polyester or glass fibers. It is composed of multiple layers of bonded materials. Technically, it's known as fiberglass reinforced plastic.

Flasher—the simplest type of depth-sounder. It uses a neon bulb to indicate the location of bottom structures.

Flats boat—a type of boat that evolved from the skiff design. It is characterized by a minimal draft and a poling platform above the outboard engine, which is used to push the boat about tidal flats while silently stalking wary fish.

Flat-V hull—see shallow-V hull.

Flotation foam—a closed-cell, polyurethane foam that is often called flotation by boat builders who use it to fill the cavities between the hull and the top deck or inner liner. The coast guard requires that boats less than twenty feet long have sufficient flotation to maintain a level attitude, even if the boat is swamped.

Flybridge boat—a type of boat with a raised bridge that is at least a full story above the main deck. It is typically smaller than a convertible, which is also equipped with a flying bridge.

Flying bridge—a helm station raised a full story above the main deck. Often called a raised bridge or a flybridge.

Four-cycle engine—a gasoline or diesel internal-combustion engine that takes four strokes of the piston to accomplish intake of fuel, compression, ignition, and discharge of exhaust.

Gaff—a pole with a metal hook end used to bring fish aboard a boat.

Gel coat—the first layer of laminate material applied to a boat mold by use of a spray gun. It is a combination of resin and pigment.

Genset—a common name for a gas or diesel electrical generator.

GPS (Global Positioning Satellite)—a radio-navigation system that works by means of an exercise in triangulation involving a network of twenty-four satellites. Receiver units must communicate with at least four satellites to obtain a location fix. Accuracy is to within about three hundred feet.

Gunwale—the upper surface on the side of a boat.

Hard chine—this occurs when the sides of the hull and the bottom intersect in a sharp angle as opposed to a curvilinear shape, which is called a rounded chine.

Hard top—a variation of the T-top that mounts a rectangle of hard fiberglass over the helm area instead of canvas. Often used as a base for an overhead platform.

Hawse pipe—a hole in a gunwale fitted with a pipe that guides lines to cleats mounted on the inside bulkhead.

Horizontal chine—similar to a strake but wider. It can be a component of a double chine.

Inboard engine—amidships-mounted, internal-combustion, four-cycle engine that runs a fixed shaft through the bottom of a hull. Can burn either gasoline or diesel fuel.

Inner liner—a fiberglass boat component that's made in a mold and joined to the hull, often as an intermediary layer below top decks and cabin superstructure. It adds structural rigidity.

Jack plate—a hydraulic or manual device installed between the transom and an outboard engine that enables a boater to move the engine vertically, up or down. It is independent of trim and is used by inshore fishermen to reduce draft for running in shallow water.

Keel—the bottom point or longitudinal centerline of a hull.

Kicker motor—a small outboard motor that supplements a larger, main engine.

Kite fishing—a technique that involves flying a kite off the transom to present bait at a distance from the boat.

Lag—to back a screwed or riveted joint with a strip of wood.

Laminate—a single layer of material used in multi-layered fiberglass construction.

LCD recorder—a paperless depth-sounder that uses a screen called a liquid-crystal display (LCD) and is equipped with memory to play back recorded sequences.

Leaning post—a wide, padded bolster installed at the helm in place of individual seats.

Loran C (acronym for *long-range navigation*)—a radio-navigation system that uses shore-based transmitters located along the United States and Canadian coastlines. Receivers measure the difference in arrival time between the signals from a master and a secondary transmitter to determine position in numbers called LOPs (lines of position) or TDs (time differences).

Marlin tower—see tuna tower.

Mat—a cloth laminate that is made of random polyester fibers pressed flat. It is often perforated to enable resin to seep through for a firm bond. It prevents the texture of woven roving (a waffle pattern) from showing through the gel coat. Also, it absorbs heat during the curing process, and adjusts to unwanted patterning caused by varying cure rates of the laminates.

Miss Chevy—a series of boats built by John Rybovich, which defined the class of the modern convertible. *Miss Chevy IV* was built in 1952 with a large flybridge deck, tuna tower, extended split sheer, and opening transom door. It pioneered many long-range fishing features.

Modified-V hull—often called a mod-V hull, it is applied to hulls with deadrises between 12° and 17°. It represents a compromise between the soft ride of a deep-V hull and the performance efficiency of a flat bottom.

Mold—a carefully constructed hollow cavity that is a mirror image of the boat's final shape. It's based on a wooden or clay model that's built to exacting specifications and polished to flawless perfection. When the model is finished, a mold is cast and the model's exact shape and smooth surface are transferred to the mold, which in turn transfers them to the finished boat.

Nibral—an alloy composed of nickel, bronze, and aluminum.

Nonskid deck—fiberglass surfaces with geometric patterns cut into the mold or a gel-coat finish that has a sandlike texture. It prevents slippage.

Notched transom—a flat, cutaway area that recesses the keel line by several inches or feet. The length of the notches are carefully calculated so that the boat still rides mostly on the V, but water flows smoothly into the setbacks. This enables the prop and drive unit to be mounted higher out of the water to reduce hydrodynamic drag.

Outboard bracket—a two- to three-foot fiberglass extender piece added to a transom at the waterline. It functions as the mounting point for outboards, either single or twin installations. A bracket performs several functions: increases hull length to improve boat performance; moves the outboard out of the way to increase fish-fighting space and reduce operating noise and fumes; adds buoyancy to the stern; and enables offshore boats to run with full, protective transoms minus cutouts and splash wells. Many boat builders build brackets into the basic hull mold.

Outboard engine—transom-mounted internal combustion gas engine that uses two cycles of the piston to accomplish intake, combustion, ignition, and exhaust. Fuel is characterized by being a mixture of gasoline and oil.

Outriggers—tall aluminum poles on either side of the boat often fitted with spreaders and tension cables to keep trolled lines from multiple rods tangle-free.

Package boat—a manufacturer-rigged boat that arrives on the showroom floor fully outfitted and ready for launching.

Pad bottom—a hull that replaces the pointed keel on a V bottom with a long, flat pad. Few fishing boats are equipped with pad bottoms, because they provide a harsh, banging offshore ride. Typically found on high-performance boats.

Pad keel—sometimes called a delta keel, it is simply a flat area on the bottom of the hull at the transom. In boats like these, the hull rises out of the water and the boat virtually rides on the small, flat pad.

Pilar—a thirty-eight-foot, dual-engine, black-hulled boat owned by Ernest Hemingway. It was built in 1934 by the Wheeler Brothers, of the Bronx, New York, and for most of three decades regularly fished the waters between the Florida Keys, Cuba, and the Bahamas, enabling her owner to set several world records and pioneer a host of design breakthroughs, such as the flying bridge, outriggers, and many others.

Pilothouse—area on a boat that fully encloses the helm. It is typically found on workboats and commercial fishing rigs. Sportfishermen use pilothouse boats to fish in all seasons and all conditions, especially in cold-water areas.

Planing hull—a type of powerboat hull that generates lift to ride on the surface of the water to reduce hydrodynamic drag. Planing hulls have the ability to run over and pass their own bow waves.

Poling platform—a key component of a flats boat, it is a small stand raised approximately three feet above an outboard motor. A fisherman stands on the platform to scout for fish and gently use a pole to maneuver the boat.

Print through—a waffle pattern found on flawed fiberglass hulls that comes from improperly masking the texture of woven roving.

Quadaxial fiberglass—fiberglass reinforcement cloth composed of glass or polyester fibers finely stitched in four directions.

Radar—an acronym that stands for *r*adio *d*etection *a*nd *r*anging. Electronic radar units provide anglers with range, bearing, speed, time to target, and a visual image of the boat's surroundings. It is extremely valuable during times of low visibility—storms, fog, and especially at night.

Resin—liquid substance that binds laminate materials together into a solid. In boat building, resins are typically the polyester or vinylester type, which means they cure through a chemical reaction caused by a catalyst and release heat. This family is also called thermosetting. Epoxy resins are rarely used in boat building.

Reverse chine—a chine that is characterized by a downward dihedral lip, which tends to throw spray away from the boat and make for a dry ride.

Rocket launcher—a common name for a vertical rod holder.

Rolled-edge skiff—a type of simple fiberglass skiff that's built without a top deck. A single mold is used and every feature is added layer upon layer. These minimal-draft boats are characterized by rolled edges finished by rubrails, instead of distinctive gunwales.

Rub rail—a protective bumper located at the point where the top deck is joined to the hull.

Salon—an enclosed lounge/dinette area within a deckhouse. It is typically carpeted and air conditioned.

Scope ratio—the length of anchor line in relation to the depth of the water. For 100-percent holding power, the recommended scope ratio is about 7:1. Reducing the scope ratio decreases the anchor's holding power, but most fishermen use a 4:1 ratio or less in many situations.

Shallow-V hull—sometimes called a flat-V hull, it generally has a deadrise of less than 12°. It is often used on inshore boats, which require minimal draft and have little need for soft, knifelike penetration of offshore waves.

Sheer—the line the gunwales follow as they run fore and aft. In most boats, it is either straight or a graceful curve upward as it moves forward.

Shore-power hookup—an electrical connection that enables boats to tap into land-based AC power while at the dock.

Side console—a side-mounted control unit, typically affixed to the starboard gunwale.

Side deck—a dedicated catwalk deck on the outside perimeter of a cabin boat.

Skiff—a small, simple boat. The name is applied loosely to sailboats, powerboats, and rowboats.

Sonar—an acronym that stands for *so*und *na*vigation and *r*anging. The technology is used in depth-sounders, which convert electrical impulses into sound waves and transmit them into the water by means of a transducer mounted on the bottom of the hull. When the sound waves strike an obstacle and bounce back, the time difference between the transmitted signal and the received echo is measured. From this the distance to the object is determined.

Split sheer—occurs when the sheer line sharply splits amidships and produces two different sheer lines fore and aft. It is common in convertibles and other offshore boats.

Spotting platform—a welded-aluminum tower with a raised platform and belly rails. If is often equipped with a second set of helm controls.

Spring line—a line connected amidships running aft. It is used to secure a boat at the dock. The cleat that the line ties to is called a spring-line cleat.

SSB radiotelephone—stands for single-sideband high seas radiotelephone, a long-range communications link.

Stem—the bottom forward portion of the hull.

Sterndrive engine—a propulsion system composed of an inboard, automotive, four-cycle gas engine that's marinized and mounted just inside the transom. It's mated to an outdrive unit that can be trimmed up or down. Also called an I/O engine.

Strakes—sometimes called lifting or running strakes, they are elongated protrusions that run on both sides of the keel, either the entire length from stem to stern or part way. Combined with the keel, strakes help minimize roll and maintain directional tracking when underway. Combined with hard chines, they help throw spray away from the boat.

Stringers—an internal support system that helps a boat maintain its shape and structural integrity. Stringers are typically composed of one or two sets of wooden planks or rolls of fiberglass reinforcing cloth that run along the base of the hull from stem to stern. They are held in place by cross members.

Tackle-rigging station—an integrated unit that has a cutting board and room to spread out hooks, leader, sinkers, and so forth.

Tiller-handle outboard—the original method for steering and controlling throttle position for an outboard motor. It is still used on small, low-horsepower engines.

Torque—a twisting, power-delivery motion imparted to the boat by the drive shaft and prop.

Tower—a welded-aluminum structure built above the main deck or raised bridge deck. It is used to mount overhead protection and a weight-bearing platform, which fishermen use as a scanning platform when searching for fish.

Transom—a transverse bulkhead located at the stern of a boat.

Triaxial fiberglass—fiberglass reinforcement cloth composed of glass or polyester fibers finely stitched in three directions.

Tri-hull—a snub-nosed planning hull characterized by three side-by-side V-shaped bottom components. Also called a cathedral hull.

Trim—an engine adjustment that involves swinging the prop and lower gearcase up or down in an arc.

Trim tabs—twin planes located at the bottom of the

Bow-up ride is caused by excessive engine trim. Bow-down ride is caused by trimming too far under. To produce a level running attitude, a boat must be correctly trimmed.

transom that are hydraulically activated to control the running attitude of a boat.

Trolling—an offshore fishing technique that's done from a slowly moving boat that trails a pattern of natural and/or artificial bait. It enables fishermen to cover a sizable area of water for bait presentation.

T-top—the simplest aluminum tower, it provides overhead protection for the helm.

Tuna tower—the tallest and most complex aluminum tower, it frequently rises several stories above the main deck and includes a second helm station. Somewhat smaller structures are called marlin towers.

Two-cycle engine—a power plant that uses two cycles or strokes of the piston to accomplish intake, compression, ignition, and exhaust.

Unidirectional fiberglass—fiberglass reinforcement cloth composed of long glass or polyester fibers stitched together in a flat, unwoven bundle.

Variable-deadrise hull—a hull characterized by different angles of deadrise between each strake. Usually, the sharpest angles of deadrise occur nearest the chines. Raymond Hunt popularized this design, which is sometimes called a progressive-V.

V berth—a berth located below the foredeck at the bow. It is triangular in shape.

VHF—an abbreviation for very high frequency. It is a link (in the form of a system of electronic transmitters and receivers) that connects fishermen to other boats, marinas, weather channels, and the coast guard. It is technically referred to as VHF-FM radio.

V hull—the most common planing hull, characterized by a classic wedge-shaped bottom.

Video depth-sounder—similar to an LCD recorder except that it uses a cathode-ray tube instead of an LCD.

Walkaround—a type of boat that derives its name from the craft's layout, which allows fishermen to walk and fish easily around a cabin boat's outer perimeter. The chief characteristics are side decks that have nonskid surfaces, and are protected by raised hull sides and gunwales. They are also located within a step or two of the level of the aft cock-

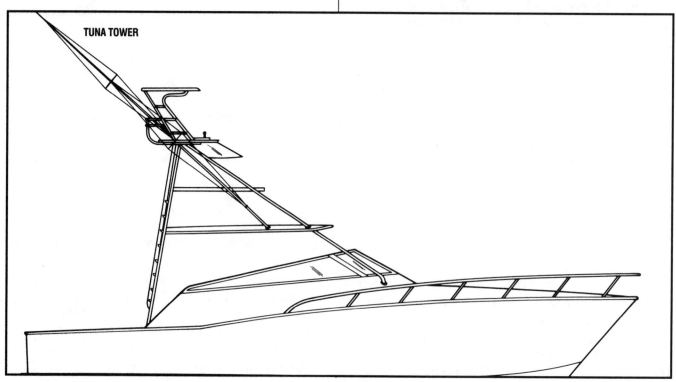

TUNA TOWER

Deep, protected perimeter decks encircle the cabin on a walkaround boat and lead to a foredeck area that can be used for bow fishing.

pit. These same characteristics are extended to the foredeck.

Windlass—an electric or manual winch-type device used to hoist an anchor.

Woven roving—the most common type of fiberglass reinforcement, which comes in clothlike sheets. It is a rough cloth of polyester or glass fibers stitched into an over-and-under, basket-weave pattern.

INDEX

Acanthocybium solandri (wahoo; oahu; Pacific kingfish), 99
accessories, 76–79
African pompano (*Alectis ciliaris*), 104
aft cabins, 38, 111
albacore (*Thunnus alalunga*), 98
Albula vulpes (bonefish), 108
Alectis ciliaris (African pompano), 104
Alopias vulpinus (thresher shark), 106
aluminum skiffs, 64–65
American Fisheries Society, 94
anchoring, 81 – 84
    retrieval and, 83–84
    scope ratio and, 82–83, 116
anchor winches, 79
angle of rode, 83
anodes, zinc, 92
Aquasport, 17, 29
Archosargus probatocephalus (sheepshead), 109
Atlantic bonito (*Sarda sarda*), 107
Atlantic cod (*Gadus morhua*), 102
Atlantic salmon (*Salmo solar*), 106–107
Atractoscion nobilis (white sea bass), 101
autopilots, 75

backing-down, 86, 87, 111
bait freezers, 76
barracudas, 108, 109
bass, sea, 101–102
battery:
    charger for, 76
    isolated, 77
    maintenance of, 89
bay boats, 63
belly, 88, 111
belly rails, 20, 111
belts, 89
Bertram company, 42
biaxial fiberglass, 5, 111
bigeye tuna (*Thunnus obesus*), 98
bilge areas, 89, 111
bilge pumps, 22, 27, 34
billfish, 95–97
Bimini tops, 19–20, 22, 36, 37, 59, 63, 78, 111
black drum (*Pogonias cromis*), 100–101
blackfin tuna (*Thunnus atlanticus*), 98
blackfish (*Tautoga onitis*), 110
black grouper (*Mycteroperca bonaci*), 102
black marlin (*Makaira indica*), 95–96

black porgy (*Tautoga onitis*), 110
black sea bass (*Centropristes striatus*), 101
bluefin tuna (*Thunnus thynnus*), 97–98
bluefish (*Pomatomus salatrix*), 107–108
blue marlin (*Makaira nigricans*), 95
blue shark (*Prionace glauca*), 106
boat handling, 81–89
　anchoring and, 81–84
　backing down and, 86, 87, 111
　chum line and, 87
　deep jigging and, 88
　fish-fighting plan and, 86–87
　fishing rules of the road and, 86–87
　flats fishing and, 88
　kite fishing and, 88–89
　line retrieval and, 87–88
　setting hook and, 89
　trolling and, 84–86
bolsters, 78
bonefish (*Albula vulpes*), 108
bonito, 107
bonito shark (*Isurus oxrhynchus*), 105
Boston Whaler, 15–16, 29
bottom scrubbing, 89–90
bow pulpit, 36, 37
brown shark (*Carcharhinus milberti*), 106

cabins, 39
　aft, 38, 111
　of walkaround boats, 36–38
calico bass (*Paralabrax clathratus*), 101
California barracuda (*Sphyraena argentae*), 108
California halibut (*Paralichthys californicus*), 103
California sheepshead (*Semicossyphus pulcher*), 108
canary rockfish (*Sebastes pinniger*), 108
canvas covers, 90
Caranx hippos (jack crevalle), 104
carbon monoxide detectors, 77
Carcharhinus milberti (sandbar shark; brown shark),
　106
Carcharhinus obscurus (dusky shark), 106
Carcharodon carcharias (white shark; great white
　shark), 106
catamaran, 11–12, 111
cathedral hull, 16, 118
CB (citizens band) radios, 75
cellular phones, 75

center console boats, 15–27, 111
　basic features of, 18–19, 22
　canvas covers for, 90
　characteristics of, 17–18
　controls of, 17–18
　express boat and, 60
　fighting chair for, 76
　large, 25–27
　layout of, *20, 25*
　midsize, 22–25
　small, 21–22
　see also pilothouse fishing boats
Centropomus undecimalis (snook), 109
Centropristes striatus (black sea bass), 101
cero mackerel (*Scomberomorus regalis*), 100
channel bass (*Sciaenops ocellatus*), 100
Chapman Piloting, 81
chart plotter, 73, 111
chart recorders, 74, 111
chines, 9–10, 112
chinook salmon (*Oncorhynchus tshawtyscha*), 107
chopped fiberglass, 5, 112
chopper gun, 4, 5
chum line, 87
chumming, 88, 112
chunking, 88, 112
cigliatera poisoning, 103, 109
citizens band (CB) radios, 75
coaming, 22, 112
cobia (*Rachycentron canadum*), 108
cockpit, 33, 58, 59, 66
　of convertible sportfishermen, 46–47
　of express boat, 61
　of walkaround boats, 34–35
cod, 102–103
coho salmon (*Oncorhynchus kisutch*), 107
*Common and Scientific Names of Fishes from the United
　States and Canada,* 94
communications, 74–75
companionway, 33–34, 112
compasses, 76
COMSAT (Communications Satellite Corporation), 75
constant deadrise, 11
convertible sportfishermen boats, 41–53, 112
　canvas covers for, 90
　cockpit of, 46–47
　design and development of, 41–44

dual controls of, 50
equipment of, 52–53
fishing rule of the road and, 86
flybridge of, 44–45
foredeck of, 51
helm stations in, 45–46
hull configuration of, 53
instruments and gauges of, 56
large, 51–53
layout of, *49, 50,* 51
multiple decks of, 46–47
prerigging of, 70
profile of, *47*
small, 48–51
tuna tower of, *45,* 46
coring material, 5, 112
Coryphaena hippurus (dolphin; dorado; mahimahi),
108–109
counter rotation, 12, 112
crow's nest, 46, 50
cuddy cabin, 27, 65, 112
cuddy-cabin boats, 31, 38–40, 64–65
cure, 112
curtains, 20, 76, 112
Cynoscion nebulosus (spotted sea trout), 101
Cynoscion regalis (weakfish), 100

DBR (Differential Beacon Receivers), 71–72
deadrise, 9, 10, 112
constant, 11
variable, 11
deckhouse, 47, 67
deep jigging, 88, 112
deep-V hull, 10, 12, 17, 25, 112
Defense Department, U.S., 71
delta keel, 11, 115
depth sounder, 73–74, 112
diesel engines, 14, 37, 112
Differential Beacon Receivers (DBR), 71–72
Differential GPS (Global Positioning Satellite), 71–72,
112
displacement, 53, 112
displacement hulls, 8, 112
dolphin (*Coryphaena hippurus*), 108–109
dorado (*Coryphaena hippurus*), 108–109
double chine, 10, 112
Down East boats, 66

downriggers, 25, 76, 112, *113*
drifting, 88
drum, 100–101
dual-console boats, 62–63, 112–113
dusky shark (*Carcharinus obscurus*), 106

electrical outlets, 90
electrolysis, 92
electronics:
fishing, 73–74
navigational, 71–73
operation/safety, 74–75
emergency position indicating radiobeacon (EPIRB),
75, 113
engines, 12–14
for center console boats, 22–23, 25–27
of cuddy-cabin boats, 39
diesel, 14, 37, 112
of dual-console boats, 62–63
of express boat, 61
of flats boat, 57–58
of flybridge sportfishermen, 67
four-cycle, 12, 14, 113
inboard, 14, 34, 114
of large convertible, 53
outboard, *see* outboard engines
of pilothouse boats, 66
of skiffs, 64
of small convertible, 48
of small walkaround, 34
sterndrive, 12–14, 26, 34, 37, 116–117
two-cycle, 12, 119
Epinephelus itajara (jewfish), 102
Epinephelus morio (red grouper), 102
Epinephelus striatus (Nassau grouper), *101,* 102
EPIRB (emergency position indicating radiobeacon),
75, 113
epoxy resins, 4, 116
equipment, 76–79
Euthynnus alletteratus (little tuna; little tunny; false albacore), 99
Evinrude, Ole, 12
express boats, 55–56, 59–62, 113
canvas covers for, 90
center console boats and, 60
characteristics of, 59–61
cockpit of, 61

express boats *(continued)*
   fishing rules of the road and, 86
   layout of, *60*
   prerigging of, 70
   profile of, *60*

false albacore (*Euthynnus alletteratus*), 99
Federal Communications Commission (FCC), 75
fiberglass, 3–7, 113
   biaxial, 5, 111
   chopped, 5, 112
   maintenance of, 91
   quadaxial, 5, 115
   reinforcement of, 5–6
   triaxial, 5, 117
   unidirectional, 5, 119
   woven roving, 5, 119
fighting chairs, 76
fire extinguisher systems, 76
fish anatomy, *94*
fish boxes, 76
fish-finder, 73
flashers, 74, 113
flats boats, 55–59, 113
   console of, 58–59
   evolution of, 56–57
   features of, 57–59
   layout of, *57*
   profile of, *56*
flats fishing, 88
flat-V hull, 10, 113, 116
Florida pompano (*Trachinotus carolinus*), 104
flotation foam, 6, 31, 113
   development of, 15–17
flounder, 103
fluke, 103
fluke anchor, *82*
flybridge sportfishermen boats, 48, 67, 113
flying bridge, 37, 113
   of convertible boat, 44–45
four-cycle engine, 12, 14, 113
freezers, for bait, 76
freshwater washdown, 90
fuel containers, *90,* 91
fuel-flow meters, 75

Gadus morhua (Atlantic cod), 102

gaff, 35, 113
gag grouper (*Mycteroperca microlepis*), 102
galley, 47, 61, 67
gasoline vapor detectors, 77
gear, 76–79
gel-coat, 4–5, 113
   maintenance of, 91
genset, 49, 113
giant mackerel (*Scomberomorus cavalla*), 99–100
giant sea bass (*Stereolepis gigas*), 101
GPS (Global Positioning Satellite) system, 70–71,
   112–114
   Differential, 71–72, 112
grab handle, 37
Grady-White, 29, 30
Gray, Zane, 41
great barracuda (*Sphyraena barracuda*), 109
greater amberjack (*Seriola dumerili*), 103–104
great hammerhead shark (*Sphyrna mokarran*), 106
Great Lakes boats, 66
great white shark (*Carcharodon carcharias*), 106
groupers, 102
gunwale, 18, 35, 114
   of flats boat, 58
   sheer of, 24
   walkable, 31–32

haddock (*Melanogrammus aeglefinus*), 103
hake, 103
halibut, 103
hammerhead shark, 106
hard chines, 9, 114
hard top, 20, 114
hardware, 91
Hatteras Yachts, 42
hawse pipes, 22, 114
Hemingway, Ernest, 1–3, 14, 41, 69, 115
Hewes, Bob, 56
Hippoglossus stenolepis (Pacific halibut), 103, *104*
horizontal chines, 9–10, 114
hulls:
   catamaran, 11–12, 111
   cathedral, 16, 118
   center console boat and, 15–17
   construction of, 3–8
   of convertible boats, 53
   deep-V, 10, 12, 17, 25, 112

displacement, 8, 112
flat-V, 10, 113, 116
flotation foam design and, 15–16
modified-V, 10, 17, 25, 114
pad bottom, 11, 115
planing, 8, *9, 10,* 16, 115
progressive-V, 119
shallow-V, 10, 116
shapes of, 8–12
tri-, 16, 117–118
V-, *see* V-hull
Hunt, Raymond, 10–11, 12, 16, 119
hybrid boats, 55–56, 67
hydrodynamic drag, 8, 11

inboard engines, 14, 34, 114
INMARSAT (International Maritime Satellite
    Organization), 75
inner liners, 4, 114
inverters, 77
I/O engine, 12, 117
isolated battery systems, 77
Istiophorus platyterus (sailfish), 96–97
Isurus oxyrhynchus (mako shark; bonito shark),
    105–106

jack crevalle (*Caranx hippos*), 104
jack plates, 14, 114
jacks, 103–105
Jersey sea skiff, 65
jewfish (*Epinephelus itajara*), 102
jigging, 88, 112

Katsuwonus pelamis (skipjack tuna; striped tuna;
    watermelon tuna), 98–99
keel, 9, 114
    delta, 11, 115
    pad, 11
kelp bass (*Paralabrax clathratus*), 101
kicker motor, 23, 114
Kiekhaeffer, Carl, 12
kingfish (*Scomberomorus cavalla*), 99–100
king mackerel (*Scomberomorus cavalla*), 99–100
king salmon (*Oncorhynchus tshawtyscha*), 107
kite fishing, 88–89, 114

lag, 8, 114

laminate, 3–6, 114
LCD recorders, 74, 114
leaning posts, 24, 114
lemonfish (*Rachycentron canadum*), 108
Lewis, Bob, 88
Life, 16
lights, 77
ling (cobia; red hake), 103, 108
lingcod (*Ophiodon clongatus*), 109
little tunny (*Euthynnus alletteratus*), 99
live wells, 24–25, 77–78
lobster boats, 66
longbill spearfish (*Tetrapturus pfluegeri*), 97
longfin tuna (*Thunnus alalunga*), 98
loran, 70–71, 72, 73, 114
Luhrs company, 42
Lutjanus campechanus (red snapper), 109

mackerel, 99–100
mahimahi (*Coryphaena hippurus*), 108
Maine boats, 66
maintenance, 89–92
Makaira indica (black marlin), 95–96
Makaira nigricans (blue marlin), 95
Mako company, 17
mako shark (*Isurus oxrhynchus*), 105–106
marlins, 95–96
marlin tower, 20, 33, 76, 114, 118
mat cloth, 5, 114
Megalops atlanticus (tarpon; silver king), 110
Melanogrammus aeglefinus (haddock), 103
Mercury Marine, 12
Merluccius bilinearis (silver hake; whitefish), 103
Miss Chevy II, 43, 114
Miss Chevy IV, 43
modified-V hull, 10, 17, 25, 114
mold, 4, 114–115
mooring ball, 83–84
Morone saxatilis (striped bass; rockfish), 109–110
Mycteroperca bonaci (black grouper), 102
Mycteroperca microlepis (gag grouper), 102
Mycteroperca nenenosa (yellowfin grouper), 102

Nassau grouper (*Epinephelus striatus*), *101,* 102
navigation electronics, 70–73
Nibral, 48, 115
nonskid surfaces, 21, 115

notched transom, 11, 115

oahu (*Acanthocybium solandri*), 99
Oncorhynchus kisutch (coho salmon), 107
Oncorhynchus nerka (sockeye salmon), 107
Oncorhynchus tshawtyscha (chinook salmon; king salmon), 107
open express boat, 59
Ophiodon clongatus (lingcod), 109
outboard brackets, 13–14, 37, 76, 115
outboard engines, 12–13, 115
    in center console boats, 22–23, 25
    problems with, 14
    twin, 25–26
Outboard Marine Company, 12
outriggers, 20, 32–33, 78, 115

Pacific halibut (*Hippoglossus stenolepis*), 103, *104*
Pacific kingfish (*Acanthocybium solandri*), 99
package boat concept, 69–70, 115
pad-bottom hulls, 11, 115
padded coaming bolsters, 78
pad keel, 11, 115
Paralabrax clathratus (kelp bass; calico bass), 101
Paralichthys californicus (California halibut), 103
Paralichthys dentatus (summer flounder), 103
pedestal seats, 78
permit (*Trachinotus falcatus*), 104
Pilar, 1–3, 14, 44, 69, 115
pilothouse boats, 55, 65–66
planing hulls, 8, *9, 10,* 16, 115
pocket convertibles, 48
Pogonias cromis (black drum), 100–101
poling platform, 57, 115
pollock (*Pollachius virens*), 102–103
polyurethane foam, 6
Pomatomus salatrix (bluefish), 107–108
pompano, 104
porgies, 109, 110
prices:
    of diesel engines, 14
    of dual-console boats, 62–63
    of express boats, 61
    of flats boats, 58
    of large convertibles, 53
    of loran units, 71
    of pilothouse boats, 66

    of rolled-edge skiffs, 64
    of small convertibles, 48–49
print through, 5, 115
Prionace glauca (blue shark), 106
progressive-V hull, 119
propulsion systems, *see* engines
Pseudopleuronectes americanus (winter flounder), 103

quadaxial fiberglass, 5, 115

Rachycentron canadum (cobia; lemonfish; ling), 108
radar, *72, 73,* 75, 116
radios, 74–75, 119
red drum (*Sciaenops ocellatus*), 100
redfish (*Sciaenops ocellatus*), 100
red grouper (*Epinephelus morio*), 102
red hake (*Urophycis chuss*), 103
red snapper (*Lutjanus campechanus*), 109
resins, 4, 5, 116
reverse chine, 9, 116
rockfish (*Morone saxatilis*), 109
rod holders (rocket launchers), 18, 22, 116
    pivoting, 78
rod racks, 78
rolled-edge skiffs, 55, 63–65, 116
    layout of, *64*
rub rail, 8, 116
rust, 91
Rybovich, Emil, 42
Rybovich, John, 41–44
Rybovich, Tommy, 42
Rybovich and Sons, 3, 42

SA (Selective Availability), 71
sailfish (*Istiophorus platyterus*), 96–97
salmon, 106–107
salmon boats, 66
Salmo solar (Atlantic salmon), 106–107
salon, 43, 116
sandbar shark (*Carcharhinus milberti*), 106
Sarda sarda (Atlantic bonito), 107
scalloped hammerhead shark (*Sphyrna lewini*), 106
Sciaenops ocellatus (red drum; channel bass; redfish), 100
Scomberomorus cavalla (king mackerel; giant mackerel; kingfish), 99–100
Scomberomorus maculatus (Spanish mackerel), 100

Scomberomorus regalis (cero mackerel), 100
scope ratio, 82–83, 116
sea bass, 101–102
Sebastes pinniger (canary rockfish), 108
Selective Availability (SA), 71
Semicossyphus pulcher (California sheepshead), 108
Seriola dumerili (greater amberjack), 103–104
Seriola laladi dorsalis (yellowtail), 104–105
shallow-V hull, 10, 116
sharks, 105–106
sheepsheads, 108, 109
sheer, 24, 116
   split, 27
sheer line, 37, 65
shore-power hookup, 38, 78, 116
shortbill spearfish (*Tetrapturus angustirostris*), 97
side consoles, 17, 116
side decks, 31–32, 116
silver hake (*Merluccius bilinearis*), 103
silver king (*Megalops atlanticus*), 110
single-sideband high seas (SSB) radiotelephone, 75,
   116
siphons, siphoning, *90, 91*
skiffs, 17
   aluminum, 64–65
   Jersey sea, 65
   rolled-edge, 55, 63–65, *64,* 116
   wooden, 64–65
skipjack tuna (*Katsuwonus pelamis*), 98–99
Slane, Willis, 42
smooth hammerhead shark (*Sphyrna gaena*), 106
snook (*Centropomus undecimalis*), 109
sockeye salmon (*Oncorhynchus nerka*), 107
sonar, 73–74, 116
Spanish mackerel (*Scomberomorus maculatus*), 100
spare parts, 91
spearfish, 97
Sphyraena argentae (California barracuda), 108
Sphyraena barracuda (great barracuda),109
Sphyrna gaena (smooth hammerhead shark), 106
Sphyrna lewini (scalloped hammerhead shark), 106
Sphyrna mokarran (great hammerhead shark), 106
splashboard, 22
splash well, *13*
split console, *see* dual console boats
split sheers, 27, 116
sports-specific design, *x*

spotted sea trout (*Cynoscion nebulosus*), 101
spotting platform, 20, 33, 36, 116
spring line, 35, 116
SSB (single–sideband high seas) radiotelephone, 75,
   116
star trolling pattern, *84*
stem, 10, 116
Stereolepis gigas (giant sea bass), 101
sterndrive engines, 12–14, 26, 34, 37, 116–117
stowage compartments, 25
strakes, 10, 11, 117
Strang, Charles, 12
stringer systems, 6, 117
striped bass (*Morone saxatilis*), 109–110
striped marlin (*Tetrapturus audax*), 96
striped tuna (*Katsuwonus pelamis*), 99
summer flounder (*Paralichthys dentatus*), 103
sunshades, 78
surfacing agent, 5
swordfish (*Xiphias gladius*), 97

tackle drawers, 78
tackle rigging station, 18, 78, 117
tarpon (*Megalops atlanticus*), 110
tautog (*Tautoga onitis*), 110
teak trim, 91–92
Tetrapturus albidus (white marlin), 96
Tetrapturus angustirostris (shortbill spearfish), 97
Tetrapturus audax (striped marlin), 96
Tetrapturus pfluegeri (longbill spearfish), 97
thermosetting, 4
thresher shark (*Alopias vulpinus*), 106
Thunnus alalunga (albacore; longfin tuna), 98
Thunnes albacares (yellowfin tuna), 98
Thunnus atlanticus (blackfin tuna), 98
Thunnus obesus (bigeye tuna), 98
Thunnus thynnus (bluefin tuna), 97–98
tiller-handle controls, 17, 117
tools, tool kit, 92
tops, 32–33, 61
torque, 17–18, 117
towers, 19–20, 32–33, 36, 117
   aluminum, 76
Trachinotus carolinus (Florida pompano), 104
Trachinotus falcatus (permit), 104
transom door, 43
transoms, 6, 117

transoms *(continued)*
  cutaway, *13,* 24
  notched, 11, 115
  of walkaround boats, 34, 37
Transportation Department, U.S., 91
triaxial fiberglass, 5, 117
tri-hull, 16, 117–118
trim, 14, 18, 118
trim tabs, 18, 23–24, 78, 87, 118
Trojan company, 42
trolling, 118
  chumming and, 88
  lures and, 85
  patterns of, 84, *84, 85*
  speed and, 85, 86
  wake characteristics and, 85
trolling motors, 78
trout, 101
T-top, 20, 36, 63, 76, 118
tunas, 97–99
tuna tower, 20, 33, *45,* 46, 61, 76, 118
twin engines, 25–26
two-cycle engines, 12, 119

unidirectional fiberglass, 5, 119
Urophycis chuss (red hake; ling), 103, 108
Urophycis tenuis (white hake), 103

vapor detectors, 77
variable deadrise, 11, 119
varnish, 91–92
V berth, 35, 38, 61, 119
vertical jigging, 88
VHF radio, 74–75, 119
V hull, 9–10, 15, 17, 34, 37, 39, 61, 66, 67, 119
  diesel engine and, 14
video depth–sounders, 74, 119
Viking company, 42
Volvo Penta, 12
V trolling pattern, *84*

wahoo (*Acanthocybium solandri*), 99
wake characteristics, 85
walkaround cabin boats, 29–38, 119
  cabin of, 36–38
  canvas covers for, 90
  characteristics of, 29–31

  cockpit of, 34–35
  cuddy cabin of, 32
  cuddy-cabin boats and, 38
  derivation of, 29–31
  features of, 32–34
  fighting chair for, 76
  large, 37–38
  layout of, 31–32
  small, 35–37
washdown, 90
watermelon tuna (*Katsuwonus pelamis*), 99
water-temperature gauges, 78–79
wax, 4, 91
weakfish (*Cynoscion regalis*), 100
Wheeler Brothers, 1, 115
whitefish (*Merluccius bilinearis*), 103
white hake (*Urophycis tenuis*), 103
white marlin (*Tetrapturus albidus*), 96
white sea bass (*Atractoscion nobilis*), 101
white shark (*Carcharodon carcharias*), 106
windlasses, 37, 79, 119
winter flounder (*Pseudopleuronectes americanus*), 103
wood, 3, 5–6, 8
wooden skiffs, 31, 38–40, 64–65
workboat, 65
World Fishes Important to North Americans, 94
World Record Game Fishes, 94
woven roving fiberglass, 5, 119
W trolling pattern, *84*
Wynne, Jim, 12

Xiphias gladius (swordfish), 97

yellowfin grouper (*Mycteroperca nenenosa*), 102
yellowfin tuna (*Thunnes albacares*), 98
yellowtail (*Seriola laladi dorsalis*), 104–105

zinc anodes, 92